Women's Rights and the Bible

Women's Rights and the Bible
Implications for Christian Ethics and Social Policy

RICHARD H. HIERS

With a foreword by Lisa Sowle Cahill

PICKWICK *Publications* · Eugene, Oregon

WOMEN'S RIGHTS AND THE BIBLE
Implications for Christian Ethics and Social Policy

Pickwick Publications
An Imprint of Wipf and Stock Publishers
199 W. 8th Ave., Suite 3
Eugene, OR 97401

www.wipfandstock.com

ISBN 13: 978-1-61097-627-5

Cataloguing-in-Publication data:

Hiers, Richard H.

 Women's rights and the Bible : implications for Christian ethics and social policy / Richard H. Hiers; with a foreword by Lisa Sowle Cahill.

 xxxiv + 120 p. ; 23 cm. Includes bibliographical references and indexes.

 ISBN 13: 978-1-61097-627-5

 1. Women in the Bible. 2. Bible and law. 3. Women—Legal status, laws, etc.—Middle East. I. Title.

BS1199.W7 H54 2012

Manufactured in the U.S.A.

A good wife who can find?
　　She is far more precious than jewels.
She opens her hand to the poor,
　　and reaches out her hands to the needy.
She opens her mouth with wisdom,
　　And the teaching of kindness is on her tongue.
Her children rise up and call her blessed;
　　her husband also, and he praises her.

　　　　　　　　　　　—Proverbs 31:10, 20, 26, 28

Contents

Foreword

CHRISTIAN ADVOCATES OF GENDER equality have always had an uneasy relationship with the Bible. The nineteenth-century campaigner for women's suffrage, Elizabeth Cady Stanton, declared, "The Bible and the church have been the greatest stumbling block in the way of women's emancipation." Most Christians today would immediately recognize the "usual suspects" motivating such a critique, whether they agree with it or not: the New Testament "household codes" telling wives to be submissive to their husbands (Eph 5:21—6:9; Col 3:18—4:1; Titus 2:1-10; 1 Pet 2:18—3:7); and in the Old Testament, the fact that God's promises are handed down through the "patriarchs"—Abraham, Isaac, and Jacob—while their wives, the "matriarchs," are denied equal mention (e.g., Gen 35:11-12; Exod 3:6, 13-16; Acts 7:32).

In recent decades, biblical scholar Phyllis Trible has exposed even more shocking biblical texts condoning rape and anti-woman mayhem as "texts of terror."[1] Fortunately, liturgical readings and Sunday school books do not typically rehearse for the Christian faithful the stories of Jephthah's sacrifice of his virgin daughter in gratitude for having won a battle (Judg 11:21-40); the rape and dismemberment of a Levite's concubine (Judg 19:1-30); or the rape of King David's daughter Tamar by her half-brother Amnon (2 Sam 13:1-22). The coerced sex and pregnancy endured by the slave girl Hagar at the hands of the couple Abraham and Sarah (Gen 16:1-16; 21:9-21) is reminiscent of the present-day kidnapping and bondage of girls like Elizabeth Smart and Jaycee Dugard. Yet in most retellings (at least by middle-class white Christians) Hagar appears as a mere footnote to the blessing of Abraham and Sarah with the birth of their son Isaac. Despite our collective and selective amnesia about biblical degradations of women, the ethos out of which they came has left its mark. As Trible exclaims in introducing the Levite's

---

1. Phyllis Trible, *Texts of Terror: Literary-Feminist Readings of Biblical Narratives* (Philadelphia: Fortress, 1984).

concubine, "The betrayal, rape, torture, murder, and dismemberment of an unnamed woman is a story we want to forget but are commanded to speak. It depicts the horrors of male power, brutality, and triumphalism; of female helplessness, abuse, and annihilation. To hear this story is to inhabit a world of unrelenting terror that refuses to let us pass by on the other side."[2]

Both Stanton and Trible are ardent advocates of women's welfare, rights, and inherent value quite independently of any relation to a man. Yet they not only remained life-long Christians, they even continued to turn to the Bible for inspiration precisely in their quest for women's equality in church and society! Stanton led a team of biblical revisionists who took from the Bible excerpts that either portray women badly or fail to mention them, then supplied an original reconstruction or reinterpretation that could back women's dignity and rights. The result was *The Woman's Bible* (1895, 1898), the importance of which was denied recognition by professional biblical scholars, but which became a best-seller in Stanton's own day.[3] Trible published a landmark book in feminist biblical interpretation in the 1970s, arguing, for example, from textual evidence that the Genesis creation stories in no way hold or imply that the first woman was created to be lesser than or subservient to the first man, or that women's subordination to men after "the Fall" is divinely mandated and perpetual.[4] These texts counterbalance the texts of terror and should govern Christian gender relations and gender politics.

An important aspect of Christian feminist theology is that, almost by definition, it uses some parts of the tradition to critique and revise others. For example although Colossians 3:18 tells women to be subject to their husbands, Paul in Galatians 3:28 announces that, in the Lord, there is no male or female. Although Hagar was treated unjustly by her masters, Deborah was a leader in her own right, a prophet and a judge (Judg 4:4). Although Genesis does not treat the patriarchs and matriarchs

---

2. Trible, *Texts of Terror*, 65.

3. A handwritten manuscript of *The Woman's Bible* is in the Library of Congress. The manuscript draft held by the Library contains only Stanton's contributions and consists of passages from the books of Genesis, Exodus, and Numbers, published in *The Woman's Bible, Part I*, and from Matthew, published in *The Woman's Bible, Part II*. (http://lcweb2. loc.gov/cgi-bin/query/r?ammem/mcc:@field%28DOCID+@lit%28mcc/049%29%29; accessed 12/22/11).

4. Phyllis Trible, *God and the Rhetoric of Sexuality* (Philadelphia: Fortress, 1978).

equally, Mary Magdalene stands out among the apostles as a first witness to the resurrection (in all four Gospels); and women exercise leadership in Paul's house churches (Chloe, Prisca, Phoebe, and Junia for example). Christian thinkers and theologians interested in gender equality necessarily select a "canon within the canon" and see the gender message of some texts as more normative than others. Such scholars even reject the normativity of gender-oppressive texts entirely, at least as far as men's and women's status is concerned.

This process of selection implies that some other standard or standards of Christian identity and theology are being used in addition to the biblical narratives. In fact, it is impossible at the practical level to define "Christian values" in terms of the Bible alone. The reason is that Scripture is always read from a particular historical, ecclesial, social, and personal standpoint. The many communities in which an interpreter participates and the influences that go to make up his or her worldview are powerful shapers of what he or she "sees" in the biblical texts and recovers "for today." Our era is one in which the equal dignity of the sexes is increasingly acknowledged, and educational, legal, and social reforms grant girls and women significant access to public roles and influence. Hence the egalitarian potential of the biblical narratives and the unacceptability of the sexist currents that still run through them have become more and more obvious.

In *Women's Rights and the Bible*, Richard Hiers adds to the resources in which Christian women and men may find a "usable past" amenable to the program of gender equality. Hiers does not deny that contrary biblical evidence exists. However, he does not dwell on it. His intention is to show that in the Old Testament or Hebrew Bible,[5] evidence in favor of women's dignity and leadership far exceeds the contrary evidence. Thus it can be and indeed is an important support to Christian advocates of women's rights. To the project Hiers brings a wealth of interdisciplinary expertise—in theology, biblical studies, and law. His scholarly acumen and his

5. In his "Preface," Hiers offers several reasons in favor of continuing to use the traditional appellation "Old Testament" (rather than Hebrew Bible or Hebrew Scriptures) for the collection under discussion. While these reasons are not unsound, I find that the term "Hebrew Bible" is useful in displacing the unfortunately well-entrenched Christian supersessionist idea that the true meaning of the "Old Testament" is ultimately contingent on the New Testament, whose christological message the former foreshadows. The Hebrew Bible (Tanakh) is in its own right the founding narrative of God's everlasting covenant with the Jewish people.

balanced judgment have already been well established. Hiers' conclusions and suggestions about the relevance of his findings for contemporary social ethics and policy also are solidly grounded in the kind of integrative study so essential to the field of Christian ethics and politics. Even feminist theologians who, like Trible, may think it salutary to linger longer with the brutal realities of biblical violence toward women will be supported in their reconstructive project by positive counterpoints Hiers uncovers to our view.

Hiers' focus is the Old Testament, rather than the New Testament, primarily because he is developing his earlier argument in *Justice and Compassion in Biblical Law* (London: T. & T. Clark, 2009). One reason is that many Christians assume wrongly that the Old Testament paints an unrelievedly negative picture of women's status. Thus they turn to the ministry of Jesus for an inclusive view of church and society without seriously investigating the riches of the older Scriptures. In addition, Hiers believes that Jesus and the early church were more interested in personal conversion and personal moral reform than in reform of social structures. The Hebrew Bible, on the other hand, urges protection of the widow, the orphan, the poor, and the stranger in the land. It is specifically structures that the prophets are addressing, and their predictions of God's wrath unleashed upon exploiters are fearsome.

While many or even most Christian social ethicists would grant that Jesus was not a social reformer in the modern sense, they would take issue with the idea that Jesus' iconoclastic table fellowship and confrontation with the Jerusalem elites had no bearing on the fate of social structures. After all, "kingdom of God" is a political metaphor and Jesus was executed by temple and Roman authorities for political reasons; labeled sarcastically "King of the Jews." Yet Hiers is certainly right to call our attention to neglected sources in the Hebrew Bible that advocate structural change clearly—and for the recalcitrant ominously—and that defend the social and legal recognition of women's dignity and agency as equal to that of men.

Indeed, here Hiers has a surprising ally in Elizabeth Cady Stanton, who in her 1848 address to the Women's Rights Convention in Seneca Falls NY, declaimed, "In every generation God calls some men and women for the utterance of truth, a heroic action, and our work today is the fulfilling of what has long since been foretold by the Prophet Joel 2:28:

'And it shall come to pass afterward, that I will pour out my spirit upon all flesh; and your sons and your daughters shall prophesy.'"[6]

Hiers' specific thesis is that biblical law grants women many of the same rights as men, and that extra-biblical cultural notions of women's native inferiority infected Christianity co-dependently with a theology that appealed to biblical texts such as Genesis 3 for validation of the normativity of women's subservience. Hiers argues to the contrary that the biblical evidence supports rights for women that are similar to those captured in modern legal categories such as "due process," "rights," "equal protection," and "legal capacity." Women in the biblical world (or at least the world portrayed by the texts) were able to enter into contracts, buy and sell land, and be beneficiaries of wills. Daughters inherited from their fathers only if there were no sons, but before other male family members. Hiers also makes the case from instances of biblical widows obviously residing in their own houses or owning property, that widows were first in line to inherit their husband's estates. And whether their stories reflect exactly or not the historical record and the actual situation of women in ancient Israel, women like Sarah, Rebekah, Ruth, Naomi, Tamar, Deborah, and Judith were women of importance and power with "independent and determined personalities." Yes, their strength and agency still took shape within systems that privileged fathers, husbands, and sons over mothers, daughters, and women. Yes, the matriarchs' determination was often aimed precisely at goals (like bearing a son) that would serve their interests and those of their families within that system. But Hiers also shows that when retrieved and revised in light of a commitment to gender equality, the Hebrew Bible's/Old Testament's vision of women's place in the world can inspire and animate the Christian case for women's rights.

Lisa Sowle Cahill
J. Donald Monan Professor, Boston College

---

6. See   http://www.thelizlibrary.org/undelete/library/library003.html   (accessed 12/22/2011).

Preface

THIS PREFACE TAKES UP three preliminary matters. The first is to identify the book's core thesis with respect to rights and legal status of
women in biblical tradition. The second is to indicate why in this book
the portion of biblical tradition commonly called "the Old Testament" is
so designated here. And the third is to point to the importance of the Old
Testament, particularly Old Testament law, as an important, though usually neglected resource for contemporary reflections on Christian ethics
and social policy.

THESIS AND SCOPE

If someone were to ask even a reasonably well-informed church go-er for
his or her views as to the topic of this book, the answer might be something like this: "Don't you know that women in the Old Testament had no
status, legal or otherwise, and, *of course*, no rights? Why bother about the
Old Testament anyhow—it's all out of date, over two or three thousand
years old. And Old Testament law is worse yet. Just a bunch of bloody
sacrifices and meaningless rituals. Nothing that could possibly relate to
life today. All we have in the Bible that might be worth thinking about are
the prophets, maybe some psalms, the sayings of Jesus, and possibly some
of the rest of the New Testament. As to the Old Testament, who needs it?"

The present book is written on the basis of the writer's conviction
that the Old Testament[1] presents many insights into matters of faith and
ethics, insights that sometimes may provide inspiration and guidance for
people living in modern times confronting not altogether different issues
and concerns. The book's main thesis is that biblical law accorded women
many of the same rights as men, and, moreover, in some ways challenges

---

1. In this book, the term "Old Testament" is often used inclusively, to include both
the writings now known as "the Old Testament" and those found in "the Old Testament
Apocrypha," also known as the "Deutero-Canonical" Scriptures, which, together,
constituted the Bible of the early Christian communities.

our own society's failure to establish legal and political structures where human beings, both male and female, can flourish and interact positively in mutually supportive communities.

Other writers have drawn attention to some of the remarkably positive characterizations of women in various parts of the Old Testament. One fine study published as long ago as 1926, *The Bible Status of Women*, by Lee Anna Starr, is cited frequently in this book, along with several more recent writings. As will be seen, biblical tradition typically portrays women as independent and resourceful personalities, and many texts express appreciation and respect for women and concern for their welfare. What the present book has to offer to current discussions of women's status in the Bible is its examination of women's rights and status according to biblical law. This is a large subject, and the present book does not attempt to consider all of its aspects. Here I undertake to classify and analyze a wide range of biblical laws using certain modern Anglo-American legal categories. I approach biblical laws regarding women in the same way as in my recent study, *Justice and Compassion in Biblical Law*. There, it turned out that several modern legal categories aptly describe a great many biblical laws: for instance, those having to do with "contracts," "torts," "capital punishment," "due process," and "social legislation." Moreover, much of biblical law involves values and goals that could be considered pertinent to reflections on social ethics in contemporary society. The principal modern legal categories explored here are "rights," "equal protection," and "legal capacity," terms and concepts to be explained in Part Two, below. Because neither Jesus nor any of the New Testament writers promulgated any *laws* or articulated any *rights*, New Testament texts are considered here only when they illustrate or otherwise relate to laws or rights set out in the Old Testament.

Before turning to the relevant texts themselves, I offer two further sets of observations. The first has to do with my reasons for using the term "Old Testament" rather than "Hebrew Scriptures." The second concerns the rather strange lack of attention to the Old Testament in the work of Christian ethicists and, related to this, offers some suggestions about the importance of the Old Testament—and even Old Testament law—as resources for Christian ethics.

OLD TESTAMENT OR HEBREW SCRIPTURES

To begin, why call these writings "the Old Testament"? The short answer might be: That's what they have always been called in English, and equivalent terms in other languages. However, it is now common, particularly in more liberal Protestant churches, to find what once was called "the Old Testament," identified instead by names like "Hebrew Scriptures" or "the Hebrew Bible." In the same circles, "the New Testament" sometimes is re-labeled "Christian Scriptures." Very likely the new nomenclature derives, at least in part, from a vague sense that liberal or progressive Christians should avoid hurting the feelings of Jewish friends by implying that "ours" is new, while theirs is old and out-dated. Such motivation is certainly commendable. There are, however, some problematic consequences.

One has to do with symmetry. If the Old Testament, most of which was written originally in Hebrew,[2] is called "the Hebrew" Scriptures, why not call the New Testament, which was written, originally, if not entirely, in Greek, "the Greek Scriptures"? Or, if the New Testament is to be called "the Christian Scriptures," why not call the Old Testament the "Jewish Scriptures"? Jews rarely refers to themselves as "Hebrews."[3] Therefore, "Hebrew Scriptures" seems an inappropriate designation for Jewish Scriptures, especially since in traditional Jewish circles, the Hebrew Bible is called something else, namely, the "*Tanakh.*"

Moreover, it is not the case that the Old Testament simply equals the Hebrew Scriptures. In most Christian churches, the Bible is read in the indigenous language of each culture or nationality. Few Christians in Great Britain or America read the Bible in Hebrew. As will be noted below, the Old Testament is not simply a translation from the Hebrew text. Again, "Hebrew Scriptures" seems a bit inapt.

In all branches of Christianity, the Bible is understood to include both "the Old Testament" and the "New Testament." For Christians to refer to the New Testament as "Christian Scriptures" (in contrast to Hebrew Scripture or the Old Testament) would imply that Christianity has abandoned the Old Testament, or ceded its contents entirely to Judaism. But

2. Except for Daniel and a few verses in other OT books, which probably were written originally in Aramaic. Most of the books in the OT Apocrypha were first written in Greek.

3. The early Israelites—or perhaps precursors to the Israelites—are characterized as "Hebrews" mainly in early biblical traditions. For instance, in Gen 39:14–17; 43:32; Exod 1:15—2:13; 5:3; 1 Sam 4:6. (See also Gen 10:25–31, cataloguing the "sons of Eber.")

Christianity has not done so. At least not officially. Christian Bibles include both "testaments."

Another difference is the fact that in Hebrew Bibles, as used in Judaism, the sequence of "books" is quite different than in Christian Old Testaments. For instance, in Christian Bibles the Old Testament begins with the Pentateuch, followed by the earlier and later history books, then the wisdom writings and Psalms, the Song of Solomon, the longer prophetic books, Daniel, and finally the "Book of the Twelve" or shorter prophets, ending with Malachi. Hebrew Bibles are organized in three parts: "the Law," "the Prophets," and "the Writings," and conclude with Chronicles.

Perhaps the most significant difference is this: while Hebrew Bibles are grounded in the Masoretic Text, understood in Judaism to preserve the original language of Scripture, most Christian Bibles, beginning with the King James Version of 1611 CE, if not earlier, and such modern translations as the Revised Standard Version and the New Revised Standard Version, are based on carefully considered scholarly judgments as to what may have constituted the earliest known version of each word of the text. For example, the RSV and NRSV translations draw not only on both the pointed and the unpointed Masoretic Texts (designated respectively MT and Heb.), but also on a variety of other ancient texts, such as the Greek Septuagint (Gk.), as well as Old Latin (OL) and Syriac versions (Syr and SyrH), the Vulgate (Vg), various Targums (Tg) and the Qumran documents (Q Ms). In addition, the scholars engaged in making these translations occasionally have to use their best judgment—or make their best guess—as to the reading of a given passage (Cn). For instance, the notes at the bottom of the biblical text for 1 Samuel 1:1—2:36 in the NRSV indicate that the text has been reconstructed by using not only the MT, but also the Gk., Syr, Q Ms versions, as well as the Vulgate and Targums (and in two instances, Cn).[4] In short, the text of the Old Testament frequently differs from that of the Hebrew Scriptures.

There is one other important difference. The Greek Septuagint and some other early Christian Bibles included a number of "books" or writings that came to be excluded from Jewish or Hebrew Scriptures. These were included in later Catholic versions as "Deutero-Canonical" writ-

---

4. These symbols (and others) are used regularly in the *NOAB-RSV* and *NOAB-NRSV* editions of the Bible to identify the sources relied on for particular translations or alternative readings.

ings, and in the King James Version as the "Old Testament Apocrypha."
These, along with a few other writings preserved in Greek Orthodox and
Slavonic Bibles are included in various modern translations. The editors
of the *NOAB-RSV* and the *NOAB-NRSV* present these several writings
or "books," respectively, as "The Apocrypha of the Old Testament" and
"The Apocryphal / Deutero-Canonical Books of the Old Testament."
To complicate matters, the *NOAB-NRSV* places these "books" in a dif-
ferent sequence from that followed in the *NOAB-RSV*. Several of these
Deutero-Canonical or Apocryphal writings from the Old Testament are
cited in the present book: 1 and 2 Esdras, Tobit, Judith, Additions to
Esther, Wisdom of Solomon, Susanna, Ecclesiasticus (or Sirach), and 4
Maccabees. Necessarily, these writings are not to be found in the Hebrew
Scriptures. Possibly for this reason, they tend to be neglected by Protestant
biblical scholars and moral theologians. Several texts in these writings are
important sources for the present study.

In summary, the terms "Old Testament" and "Hebrew Scriptures"
refer to two distinct collections of writing, which, though similar in most
respects, are structured differently, often read differently, and, in the case
of the Old Testament Apocrypha, include a number of "books" not to
be found in the Hebrew Scriptures. For these reasons, the present study
uses the term "Old Testament" rather than Hebrew Scriptures. As noted
elsewhere, quotations here are drawn from both the RSV and the NRSV,
as reproduced in the *NOAB-RSV* and *NOAB-NRSV*, respectively.

THE OLD TESTAMENT AND OLD TESTAMENT LAW
AS RESOURCES FOR CHRISTIAN ETHICS

There is reason to believe that many church people (as well as most others
in the Western world) are uninformed—or misinformed—as to the contents of the Bible, particularly, the contents of the Old Testament. When
churches do not regularly follow a lectionary, or schedule of biblical
readings from both the Old and New Testaments,[5] other readings tend
to fill the vacuum, such as selections from pop-psychology or theology
and "spirituality" literature, while sermons may draw inspiration from
personal reminiscences, blogs or other media, recent films, or at most,

---

5. For instance, the *Revised Common Lectionary*, which provides a three-year cycle
of biblical readings for Sundays and festivals of the church year. Several Christian
denominations have adopted such lectionaries.

a few favorite Bible verses. One noted biblical scholar and wise observer recently puts the matter this way:

> With a few exceptions, so-called mainline churches are shrinking in strength and substance. Moreover, I do not find them grappling with biblical hermeneutics. Instead, I find Scripture cited as illustration and jumping off place—sometimes invoked as traditionally understood and other times ignored. For churches to slight the Bible, in whatever way, leaves us without a shared narrative from which faith, ethics, and action can spring. Where there is no narrative, the church stumbles into boredom and irrelevance.[6]

Instead of engaging the narratives, imagery, and insights of their scriptural heritage, many churches drift along with the interests and fads—and the beliefs and values—of their times and places. This pattern of indifference or ignorance as to biblical tradition is understandable. Many people growing up in recent decades may have come to believe that anything traditional was by definition unimportant, or even wrong, given the state of the world as then perceived. Additionally, the Bible is not an easy read. To understand its many meanings requires intensive study, and involves learning something about its languages, various theories as to the processes by which it came to be written and edited, and acquaintance with a series of complex historical developments and periods. Although a great wealth of Bible commentaries, dictionaries, and other studies is available, this literature itself is somewhat forbidding both by its quantity and, often, its density. As one biblical author put it, referring to the situation in his own time, "Of making many books there is no end, and much study is a weariness of the flesh" (Eccl 12:12).

Yet a person does not need to be a specialized scholar in order to understand the meaning of most biblical texts. Modern translations, such as the RSV and NRSV provide reliable renderings of the earliest known manuscripts. Moreover, secondary studies, such as single- and multi-volume commentaries and Bible dictionaries, if used selectively, can provide helpful information and insights for those who take the trouble to consult them. People who take their Scripture seriously might be expected to be willing to expend the effort required to search its pages for greater understanding. Both "testaments" of the Bible have always been the foundation

---

6. Trible, "Bible in Transit," 33.

for Christian faith and ethics.[7] Christian churches and individuals who abandon their Scripture may find themselves blowing in strange winds. Because some who read this book are likely to be unfamiliar with relevant biblical texts, many of them are quoted, sometimes at length, in both the main text and footnotes.

While Christian ethicists often draw on New Testament texts, few seem to consider the Old Testament as a resource or source of inspiration and insight in regard to moral and social policy matters. Here are two illustrations. One is a recent number of the Yale Divinity School journal, *Reflections*, which was sub-captioned, "No More Excuses: Confronting Poverty."[8] It included twenty-five articles and three poems, none of which drew significantly on Old Testament texts.[9] One article is titled "The Poor We'll Always Have?,"[10] but makes no mention of either Jesus' saying in the New Testament, a saying which sometimes has been construed as justifying indifference to the needs of the poor,[11] or the text in Deuteronomy from which Jesus was quoting. The Deuteronomic text would have strongly supported the article's concern:

> If there is among you anyone in need, a member of your community in any of your towns . . . do not be hard-hearted or tight-fisted toward your needy neighbor. You should rather open your hand to him, willingly lending enough to meet the need, whatever it may be . . . For the poor will never cease out of your land; *therefore I*

---

7. Some excellent recent studies have addressed what has been called the "breach" between "biblical scholarship and the life of faith." See, e.g., Arndt, *Demanding Our Attention*; and Sharp, *Wrestling the Word*.

8. Fall, 2010.

9. The article by Dean Attridge, "Early Christians and Care of the Poor," thoughtfully cites several NT passages, but only three from the OT, and those incidentally: Isa 61:1–2 (cited by Jesus in Luke 4:18), Lev 25 ("evoked" by the Isaiah text), and Prov 19:17 (as understood during the patristic period). The article by Beckmann, "A New Exodus from Hunger," includes a very brief paragraph about the biblical Exodus, which, however, seems unrelated to the problem of hunger. (*After* the Israelites escaped from Egypt, they complained about hunger in "the wilderness," and longed for the good food they had enjoyed back in Egypt [Exod 16:2–3; 17:3; Num 11:1–15].)

10. By Arthur B. Keys, Jr.

11. Matt 26:11; Mark 14:7. Luke, whose Gospel contains several sayings clearly emphasizing the critical importance of responding helpfully, even sacrificially, to the needs of the poor and others, evidently chose to omit the saying.

> command you, You shall open wide your hand to your brother, to the
> needy and to the poor, in the land.[12]

The *Reflections* authors could have also cited many other Old
Testament texts concerning the poor, texts that can aptly be characterized
as biblical social welfare legislation.[13] But they did not do so. The second
illustration is the Program for the 2011 Annual Meeting of the Society of
Christian Ethics. None of the titles of the eighty-five sessions listed in the
program referred to the Old Testament.[14] Four touched, at least indirectly,
on New Testament texts or themes.

Nevertheless, the Old Testament has not been entirely neglected
in writings on biblical ethics. Though few in number, several excellent
studies do focus on the Old Testament.[15] Most recently, and perhaps
most passionately, is Emily Arndt's posthumously published disserta-
tion, *Demanding our Attention: The Hebrew Bible as a Source for Christian
Ethics.* Arndt observes that most of the efforts to understand the Old
Testament's relevance for contemporary Christian ethics have come from
biblical scholars.[16] Conversely, "While scholarly interest in the Bible and
ethics has grown during the last several decades, very little of this work
has been done by ethicists, and much of that has focused on the New
Testament."[17]

For two quite different reasons, the New Testament offers relatively
little guidance as to questions of ethics and social policy or social eth-

12. Deut 15:7–11, emphasis supplied. Verses 7–8 (NRSV); verse 11 (RSV).

13. See Hiers, *Justice and Compassion*, chapters 8 and 9.

14. Fifty-second Annual Meeting of the Society of Christian Ethics, Jan. 6–9, 2011,
Astor Crowne Plaza, New Orleans, Louisiana. Three of eighty-five sessions listed in its
2012 program referred to OT texts. Fifty-third Annual Meeting, Jan. 5–8, 2012, Grand
Hyatt, Washington, DC.

15. For instance, Crenshaw and Willis, eds., *Essays in Old Testament Ethics*; Malchow,
Social Justice in Hebrew Bible; Maston, *Biblical Ethics*; Pilch and Malina, *Biblical Social
Values*; and Wright, *Old Testament Ethics*, and *Walking in the Ways*.

16. Arndt points to the problem of multiple languages and complex methodologies
confronting such ethicists, and the difficulty of relating biblical norms to modern ethical
reflections. She cautions against "supersessionist interpretation," and calls for interpreters
to "consciously avoid reading the Hebrew Bible through the lens of the New Testament."
And she notes the problem of "relating to ancient and strange text as a twenty-first-
century person." *Demanding Our Attention*, 6–7. The main part of the book describes
and critiques several classic and modern interpretations of Gen 22, the story of the near
or aborted sacrifice of Isaac by his father, Abraham.

17. Ibid., 15.

ics. For one thing, in New Testament times, Rome governed Palestine and much of the rest of the Mediterranean and Near Eastern world. Both Jews and Christians were subject to Roman law. Jewish authorities had, at most, limited jurisdiction, and Christians had none. When it came to social policy, Jesus' advice was: "Render unto Caesar the things that are Caesar's."[18] Paul's was only somewhat different: "Let every person be subject to the governing authorities. For there is no authority except from God, and those that exist have been instituted by God."[19] The effect was similar: Jesus' followers and the early Christians were not called on to become involved in politics or shaping social policy. The Roman Empire was not run as a participatory democracy.

Another factor also contributed to early Christians' lack of interest in social and political affairs. Although some New Testament scholars continue to conclude otherwise, ample evidence shows that all or nearly all segments of the early Christian community, if not also Jesus himself, expected the age in which they lived to end dramatically within their own lifetimes.[20] Given this eschatological expectation, New Testament ethics was, necessarily, in Albert Schweitzer's phrase, "interim ethics," that is, ethics for the interim remaining before the coming of the kingdom of God or Messianic Age. Jesus' followers and the members of the various Christian communities of whom we learn from the New Testament were called to prepare themselves for entrance into this new Age by radical detachment and moral renewal. But they were not called on to engage in social reform, or even to begin trying to transform love into justice or social policy for the benefit of others. Nor were they called to bring or establish the kingdom of God by promoting progressive legislation. When, perhaps in the near future, God's kingdom did come, there would be no

18. Matt 22:21; Mark 12:17; Luke 20:25.

19. Rom 13:1. See also Rom 13:2–7; Tit 3:1; and 1 Pet 2:13–17. Both Paul and the author of 1 Peter were referring to the government of the Roman Empire. Note mention of "the emperor" in 1 Pet 2:13, 17. The Roman Empire and its government, of course, no longer exist. The NT writers necessarily were not considering the role of citizens in nations where government is "of, by and for the people."

20. As to the problematic implications for Christian ethics, see Wilder, *Eschatology and Ethics*; the present author's *Jesus and Ethics*, and, especially, Sanders, *Ethics in the New Testament*.

need for social reform. Then God's will would then be done on Earth, as it was being been done already in heaven.[21]

Things were quite different in Old Testament times. Although the Hebrews, Israelites, Judahites, and Jews often were subject to foreign rule during the Old Testament period, they also managed to enjoy quasi-independent national status much of the time. These were not democratic nations in any modern sense. Yet, at least in the early years of the biblical period, local judges administered justice "at the gate." Later, the people of Israel and Judah chose their first kings;[22] and then when Rehoboam, the last king to rule over the united kingdoms of Israel and Judah, decided to ignore the Northerners' (Israelites') call for relief from his oppressive policies, the Northerners rebelled, and re-established their own monarchy.[23]

Biblical law necessarily applied to a wide range of social issues. For present purposes, it is not necessary to inquire how or when biblical laws may have been set down. The traditional belief, as expressed in many biblical accounts, is that YHWH ordained the law, gave it to Moses to transmit to Israel, and this law was recited at certain periodic ceremonies and eventually written down. In fact, some of it may have been borrowed from the laws of other peoples; some of it may have been created or revised by the rulings of royal, religious, and local courts; or, perhaps drafted by unidentified legislators or "law-givers."[24] However biblical laws

21. The classic studies first so concluding were those by Johannes Weiss and Albert Schweitzer. Much of subsequent NT scholarship can be understood in large part as a series of efforts to surmount (or evade) the difficulties for faith and ethics presented by Jesus' eschatological expectations. Thus, Adolf von Harnack's effort to explain Jesus' message of the kingdom of God as meaning inner religious experience and/or social progress; Rudolf Bultmann's de-mythologizing program, with eschatology converted into a recurrent, existential crisis of decision; and C. H. Dodd's "realized eschatology" proposal. More recently, others also have undertaken to explain away or by-pass the NT's futuristic eschatology in other ways; for instance: the so-called "post-Bultmannians" or "new questers"; proponents of the extra-canonical Nag Hammadi Gnostic literature; and various—often insightful—studies by members of the West Coast "Jesus Seminar." See generally the present author's book, *Jesus and the Future*. Many of these, and other modern NT scholars and moral theologians, suggest ways that conceptions of justice or social legislation might, nevertheless, be inspired by, or extrapolated from, Jesus' sayings or "ethical teachings" and example.

22. 1 Sam 11:12–15; 2 Sam 2:1–4; 3:17–21.

23. 1 Kgs 12:1–12.

24. See, e.g., Carmichael, *Spirit of Biblical Law*.

were made, they addressed many kinds of questions that now could be characterized as matters of justice and social policy.

Many people in our time are ambivalent about law. It has been found that people's attitudes towards law are shaped by their experience with "the law"; for instance, with police officers, or with courts that may or may not have ruled in their favor.[25] Christian ethicists have given relatively little attention to biblical law.[26] Traditionally, Christians have preferred to think of themselves as living under "the gospel" and not under biblical law.[27] Ethicists sometimes refer positively to "prophetic religion," or the biblical prophets' concern for "justice" and "righteousness." Yet when biblical prophets spoke of "justice" and "righteousness," they probably intended to invoke specific biblical laws that gave effect to the values and concerns these terms represent. It is clear that a great many biblical laws can be so described.

This is not to suggest that biblical laws, without more, can or should be taken as the basis for social policy in the twenty-first century. In many ways, obviously, conditions are quite different now from those in biblical times. Nevertheless, biblical law remains a significant part of Christian Scripture. A great deal of wisdom and experience—whether divine, human, or both—may have inspired some of these laws. It is also clear that the biblical lawmakers got it wrong some of the time. Yet biblical tradition includes perspectives that provide criteria for evaluating both laws and practices, whether biblical or modern.[28] It is not so much "time" that "makes ancient good uncouth," as moral insights, some as old as the Bible

---

25. Muir, *Law and Attitude Change.*

26. See Hiers, *Justice and Compassion*, 174, note 2, naming a series of major Christian ethicists who "typically give little or no attention to biblical law in their reflections on ethics and social ethics."

27. Paul's understanding of biblical law was complex and ambiguous, but largely negative as to its continuing place in the Christian life. See, e.g., Rom 2:12—8:8 and Gal 2:2—5:14. Jesus' attitude may have been more positive, if ambivalent. See, e.g., Matt 5:17–48; 19:2–9, 16–19; Mark 10:17–22; Luke 16:16–18; 18:18–21.

28. See Otto, "False Weights," 146: "[I]f equality is a tenet of all modern concepts of law, that all humans are to be treated alike, then a decisive step into this direction was made by the Deuteronomistic concept of a society without marginalized people. The idea that individuals could change their social surroundings was not a fruit of the Renaissance but already of the Hebrew Bible."

itself, that, in time, have come to be recognized as calling into question ancient, and not so ancient, beliefs and practices.[29]

What is proposed here, is to take biblical law seriously: to try to understand the values and visions that informed biblical laws, and to keep open the possibility that some of those values and visions may be relevant to reflections on ethics and social policy issues today. It might even be just possible that people today might learn something from biblical law and tradition about the importance of women and the kinds of rights women should enjoy in our own time.[30] The next task, in any case, is to try to understand what the biblical writers themselves said, and attempt to determine what those who set down the biblical laws intended them to mean.

29. See Frymer-Kensky, "Bible and Women's Studies," 18: "It is true that many of our moral ideas ultimately come from the Bible, but it is also true that they have been inspired by our continued reflection on the Bible during the millennia since it was written." As a case in point, one might consider the inscription on the Liberty Bell in Philadelphia: "Proclaim liberty throughout the land to all the inhabitants thereof" (Lev 25:10, KJV). The cultural, social, political, and legal implications of the ideal of "liberty" continue to unfold. For instance, in the forms of religious opposition to slavery and the slave trade, then to racial segregation, and the on-going civil rights movement. In the spirit of Otto's observation quoted in the preceding footnote, it could be added that the ideal of liberty was not something first invented by eighteenth-century French *philosophes.*

30. Some specific suggestions are indicated in footnotes found in chapters 1 through 11. Chapter 13 explores three particular areas where biblical tradition and law can inform contemporary reflections on ethics and social policy.

Acknowledgments

I WISH TO EXPRESS my appreciation here for the many people whose wisdom, guidance, encouragement, and other kinds of assistance have helped me along the way in the course of my meandering journey from youthful and then "bright college" years into the fields of social ethics, religious studies, particularly "biblical theology," then later the mysterious territory of "the law," and more recently, the antique, yet sometimes strangely modern land of biblical law.

In earlier drafts of these "acknowledgements," I set out to mention all those who had helped me at particular stages of this journey. The list grew to over a hundred and fifty names, and it kept growing. Much as I would like to thank each individually, I finally decided to spare readers such an extended recitation, and also to spare those whose names otherwise would have appeared, such exposure to association with any dubious or (to use a federal appellate standard of review) "clearly erroneous" statements that may turn up in these pages. So, instead of naming many names, I simply say that I am grateful to and for:

My caring and supportive family; patient and wise teachers and mentors in early years at the Episcopal Academy; kind and insightful faculty, fellow students, administrators, and staff at Yale College, and then at Yale Divinity School and the Yale School of Graduate Studies; and thoughtful colleagues, students, and other friends in Religion and elsewhere at the University of Florida, especially my fine teachers, fellow students, colleagues, students, deans, and support personnel at the University of Florida's Levin College of Law. Also friends and colleagues at other colleges, universities, divinity schools and law schools, many of whom I have been privileged to know as fellow members of the American Academy of Religion, Danforth Associates in Teaching, the Society of Biblical Literature, the Society of Christian Ethics, and the somewhat loosely affiliated clusters of participants in a long series of annual conferences on "Law, Religion, and Ethics" at the Hamline University School of Law.

Also, several state and federal judges, particularly the late Judge Jerre S. Williams, his wise and gracious secretaries, and thoughtful fellow law clerks. And finally, the religion journal, law journal, and publishing house editors—including those at Wipf and Stock—who have been so brave (or misguided) as to publish my reflections on matters pertaining to religion, ethics, and law.

I wish to thank four people for their help in preparation of this book: Mrs. Robin M. Roundtree and Thomas G. Williams, for technical assistance and patient encouragement in the use of perennially new, and increasingly complicated word processing programs; and Christian Amondson and Dr. Robin Parry, for their guidance and excellent editorial suggestions. And I am grateful to the University of Florida for providing me with splendid research and writing facilities.

Richard H. Hiers
March 2012

Abbreviations

Add Esth	Additions to Esther
BCE	Before Common Era (BC)
CE	Common Era (AD)
1–2 Chr	1–2 Chronicles
Col	Colossians
1–2 Cor	1–2 Corinthians
Dan	Daniel
Deut	Deuteronomy
Eccl	Ecclesiastes
Eph	Ephesians
1–2 Esd	1–2 Esdras
Esth	Esther
Exod	Exodus
F.2d	Federal Reporter, Second Series
Gal	Galatians
Gen	Genesis
Gk.	Greek text
Heb	Hebrews
Heb.	Hebrew Text
Isa	Isaiah
Jer	Jeremiah
Jdt	Judith
JBL	*Journal of Biblical Literature*
Josh	Joshua
JSOT	*Journal for the Society of Old Testament*
Judg	Judges
1–2 Kgs	1–2 Kings
KJV	King James Version
Lev	Leviticus
4 Macc	4 Maccabees

Mal	Malachi
Matt	Matthew
Mic	Micah
MT	Masoretic Text
Neh	Nehemiah
NOAB-NRSV	*New Oxford Annotated Bible, New Revised Standard Version*
NOAB-RSV	*New Oxford Annotated Bible, Revised Standard Version*
NRSV	New Revised Standard Version
NT	New Testament
Num	Numbers
OT	Old Testament
1–2 Pet	1–2 Peter
Prov	Proverbs
Ps, Pss	Psalms
Rom	Romans
RSV	Revised Standard Version
1–2 Sam	1 and 2 Samuel
Sir	Sirach (Ecclesiasticus)
S.Ct.	*Supreme Court Reporter*
Song	Song of Solomon
Sus	Susanna
1–2 Tim	1–2 Timothy
Tit	Titus
Tob	Tobit
U.S.	*United States Reports*
U.S.C.	United States Code
Wis	Wisdom of Solomon
YHWH	Tetragrammaton, representing the divine name in many Hebrew texts of the OT
Zech	Zechariah

Introduction

THE CONVENTIONAL WISDOM AMONG interpreters of the Bible, including many feminist scholars, is that in biblical times women were considered inferior and subordinate to men. Commentators often assert that the Bible as a whole is androcentric or male-centered, and that women had few, if any, legal rights. Some even urge that, so far as biblical law was concerned, women were non-persons.

The idea that in biblical times wives were supposed to be submissive and subordinate to their husbands derives, at least in part, from certain Pauline, deutero-Pauline, pseudo-Pauline, and post-Pauline texts in the New Testament, notably: 1 Corinthians 11:3–18; 14:33–36; Ephesians 5:22–24; Colossians 3:18; 1 Timothy 2:11–15; Titus 2:4–5; and 1 Peter 3:1–6.[1] The idea that wives should be "subject" or subservient to their husbands seems to have been part of the emerging churches' interim ethics. Some of these NT texts cite as authority the narratives found in Genesis 2:18–22 and 3:1–6, but, curiously, do not refer to Genesis 3:16.[2] Arguably early Christian attitudes toward women were influenced more by Greco-Roman culture than by Christian Scripture, which at the time consisted largely of what we now call the Old Testament and the Old Testament Apocrypha.[3]

1. These and other NT texts have been examined carefully, with a view to their relevance for contemporary faith and understanding, e.g., by Evans, *Women in the Bible*, 61–130, and Stendahl, *Bible and Role*, 28–43. See also Starr, *Bible Status*, 177–340, an early and remarkably thorough examination of pertinent biblical texts. Compare Wacker, "Foundations," 51: "With very few exceptions such as the Song of Songs, the Bible may be spoken of in its entirety as an androcentric literature." The only biblical text Wacker cites as authority for this conclusion is 1 Tim 2:12–15.

2. Discussed below, chapter 5.

3. See Evans, *Woman in the Bible*, 38–41. It has been suggested also, that the NT texts advocating male dominance and female submission were influenced by Jewish sources, notably some of the apocryphal and pseudepigraphic writings and Haggada. See Prusak, "Women: Seduction Siren," 89–100. These Jewish sources themselves probably reflect Hellenistic influence.

The Old Testament includes stories about men abusing women, sometimes brutally and with tragic consequences. And, as will be seen, not all biblical laws accorded women the same legal rights or status as men, and some clearly failed to protect women's interests. However, the regnant hypothesis—that the Bible, as a whole, calls for women to be subservient to men—ignores the many OT texts that typically view women positively as strong and independent persons, as well as the numerous biblical laws that recognize women's legal rights.

Readers may sometimes be misled by the long-established Christian habit of reading the Old Testament through the lenses of the New Testament. In addition, historically and culturally transmitted beliefs about women's inferiority may continue to prompt readers to assume that such beliefs must have been operative back in old biblical times as well. Moreover, modern readers tend to dismiss biblical law as archaic and irrelevant, and assume that it can and should be ignored, rather than read carefully in order to learn what it actually had to say. At any rate, the question of women's legal capacity[4] in Old Testament times has received little if any attention in earlier studies.

While it is true that, according to biblical law and tradition, women were not entitled to equal protection in *all* respects, women nevertheless enjoyed considerably greater legal status than is commonly recognized. This book examines biblical traditions relating to women's legal status and rights in the Old Testament period. In particular, it focuses on biblical texts relating to women's legal capacity: notably, the rights to be treated fairly and equally under the law; to appear or testify in court; to enter into contracts; and to purchase, own, transfer, and inherit property. Readers may find both the evidence and the conclusions presented here somewhat surprising. The texts considered span the full range of the biblical period, from early times, perhaps as early as the twelfth century BCE, down to, and into the first century CE.

As background, the book begins by considering a variety of texts relating to the place of women in the several communities and eras rep-

---

4. *Black's Law Dictionary* defines legal "capacity" as follows (second definition): "The power to create or enter into a legal relation under the same circumstances in which a normal person would have the power to create or enter into such a relation; specifically, the satisfaction of a legal qualification, such as legal age or soundness of mind, that determines one's ability to sue or be sued, to enter into a binding contract, and the like." Garner, ed., *Black's Law Dictionary*, 220.

resented in Old Testament[5] times. These include texts describing the role of women in what are commonly called the stories of the "patriarchs," and in other stories about husbands and wives; stories about other women of recognized status or importance, including those for whom biblical "books" were named; and other texts reflecting a variety of attitudes towards women. These texts indicate that women were regarded more highly in biblical times than in many latter day communities that were influenced by androcentric norms and practices deriving from other sources.[6] It will be seen that, contrary to many recent interpretations, biblical wives were neither regarded as property, nor seen as subordinate or subject to their husbands, and that biblical women frequently were represented as inner-directed persons who could, and often did, act decisively on their own initiative.

Nevertheless, it is clear that women in Old Testament society generally were less in the foreground than were men. Most of the political and judicial leaders were men—whether judges, sovereign rulers, lawgivers, or elders—as were most of the prophets and wisdom authors, and all of the priests. Yet, as will be seen, a number of women were able to rise to the level of their own personal capacity to be who they were, assuming and being recognized for impressive roles of leadership and influence. These women deserve spotlight attention and honored remembrance for having done so.

---

5. The term "Old Testament" is used in this book, instead of "Hebrew Scriptures." See the preface to this book. Also, see below, chapter 3, note 23 and accompanying text. To avoid confusion, some interpreters recently have begun to use the terms "First Testament" and "Second Testament" instead of "Old Testament" and "New Testament." See, e.g., Schaberg, "The Case of Mary Magdalene," 75–76.

6. Thus also Frymer-Kensky, "Bible and Women's Studies," 26: "Much of the patriarchy that we associate with the Bible and all of its misogyny has been introduced into the Bible by later generations of readers." As will be seen below, in chapter 5, a few texts in Sirach could be said to express moments of masculinist misogyny which possibly derived from Hellenistic culture. Frymer-Kensky probably was thinking of the Hebrew Bible, which does not include Sirach, or other writings found in the OT Apocrypha.

PART I

Background: Perspectives on Women in Old Testament Times

IN RECENT YEARS BIBLICAL perspectives on women have been considered by many scholars, often in great detail.[1] Yet relatively little attention has been given to the legal status of women under biblical law. In Part I we review biblical texts that indicate ways women were regarded in Old Testament times as prelude to a closer examination of texts relating to women's *legal* status and capacity. This preliminary survey is important, because, as is generally recognized, a society's laws are typically grounded on its current and traditional attitudes and values, at any rate, those of its dominant elements.

The first four of the following chapters demonstrate that biblical women often took center stage, usually sharing the spotlight with fortunate, but also occasionally unfortunate, men. The first chapter examines relations between the so-called "patriarchs" and their wives. It is noted that the term "patriarchs" is never used in the Genesis accounts, and that their wives are never represented as being subservient to any of the men commonly so designated. The second chapter reviews other biblical stories about husbands and wives, and observes that in each case, the wives appear to have been strong and independent personalities. The third chapter identifies a number of women celebrated in biblical tradition for their important historical contributions, or for other noteworthy deeds or status.

1. See e.g., Ebeling, *Women's Lives*; Evans, *Woman in the Bible*; Frymer-Kensky, *Reading Women*; Jay, *Throughout Your Generations*; Pressler, *View of Women*; Scholz, *Women's Hebrew Bible*; Schottroff, et al., *Feminist Interpretation*; Starr, *Bible Status*; and Stendahl: *Bible and Role of Women*. See also studies, by, among others Lisa Sowle Cahill, Katie Geneva Cannon, Margaret A. Farley, Elizabeth Schüssler Fiorenza, Sallie McFague, Carol L. Meyers, Judith Plaskow, Letty M. Russell, Rosemary Radford Ruether, and Phyllis Trible.

Several women whose actions are described in biblical "books" named in honor of women are considered in chapter 4. The fifth chapter examines attitudes toward women expressed in other biblical traditions, particularly those found in laws and the wisdom books. Separate subsections of that chapter describe perspectives regarding women generally, then "loose" women, mothers, daughters, wives, and, finally, widows.

1

The So-called "Patriarchs" and their Wives

> She went to Canaan and became the wife of Isaac, and subse-
> quent events proved that she, like Sarah, was quite equal to the
> task of managing her husband.
>
> —Anna Lee Starr

THE TERM "PATRIARCH" DERIVES from Greek, and means, in effect,
"ruling father," or "father who rules." According to one of the essays
in the *New Oxford Annotated Bible*,[1] "[t]he name 'Patriarch' is given to
Abraham, Isaac, and Jacob (Israel) and his sons, for whom the twelve
tribes were named."[2] Curiously, however, these persons are not designated
anywhere in Genesis or elsewhere in Hebrew Scriptures as "patriarchs."[3]
Instead, they are characterized simply as "fathers" of their respective

1. May and Metzger, eds., *NOAB-RSV*, 1536.

2. Other commentaries and standard dictionaries commonly give similar definitions
or descriptions. See also Wacker, "Foundations," 49: "In traditional translations of the
Bible, Abraham, Isaac, and Jacob are called 'the patriarchs.'"

3. They, and also David, are so designated a few times in the NT: Acts 2:29; 7:8–9;
and Heb 7:4. The Septuagint translates various Hebrew expressions in 1and 2 Chronicles
as *patriarches* (Gk.), and the term also appears in 4 Maccabees. On "patriarchy" as a
negative concept in feminist hermeneutics, where it is associated with male domination,
androcentrism, and monotheism, see, e.g., Wacker, "Foundations," 48–51; and generally,
Fuchs, *Sexual Politics*. Fuchs writes: "The argument of this book is that the Hebrew Bible
not only presents women as marginal, it also advocates their marginality. It is not merely
a text authored by men—it also fosters a politics of male domination." Ibid., 11. For critical but appreciative overviews of feminist hermeneutics see, e.g., Sloane, "And he shall
rule," and Parry, "Feminist Hermeneutics."
This book does not attempt to determine the extent to which social structures in biblical times can be characterized aptly as "patriarchal" or all the ways these structures may
have been repressive or oppressive to women. Nor does it attempt to describe or critique
feminist hermeneutics. Focus rather is on the biblical texts themselves.

progeny.[4] Likewise, their wives are characterized as "mothers."[5] These mothers were neither remembered nor portrayed as having been subservient either to their husbands, or to their fathers. The first of these stories concerns relations between Abraham and his wife, Sarah.

Although they had been married for some time, Sarah had not yet borne any children. In order that *she* might have children, Sarah instructed Abraham to have intercourse with Hagar, her Egyptian maid, as her surrogate.[6] Later, after Hagar had conceived, Sarah thought Hagar looked at her "with contempt," and angrily addressed Abraham: "May the wrong done to me be on you! I gave my maid to your embrace, and when she saw that she had conceived, she looked on me with contempt. May YHWH judge between you and me!" (Gen 16:5). To which Abraham meekly responded, "Behold, your maid is in your power; do to her as you please." Whereupon, Sarah "dealt harshly with her, and she fled from her."[7] Asked by YHWH's angel, who found Hagar "in the wilderness," how she came to be there, Hagar answered, "I am fleeing from my mistress Sarai." The angel then told Hagar, "Return to your mistress, and submit to her" (Gen 16:8–9). The story does not say that anyone ever told Hagar—or Sarah—to submit to Abraham.

Later, after Hagar returned and her son, Ishmael, was born, Sarah saw Ishmael playing with her own son, Isaac,[8] and again gave her husband orders, this time: "Cast out this slave woman with her son; for the son

4. See e.g., Gen 17:4–5 (Abraham, "father of a multitude of nations"); 22:7; 25:19; 26:3, 18 (Abraham, father of Isaac); Gen 26:24; 27:9–10, 18–19; 28:7 (Isaac, father of Jacob), and Gen 27:30–32, 34, 38; 28:8 (Isaac, father of Esau); Gen 37:2–4, 12 (Jacob, father of Joseph and his brothers). Similarly, certain other biblical figures are said to have been "fathers" of other peoples: e.g., Gen 17:20 (Ishmael, father of twelve princes); 19:36–38 (Lot, father of Moabites and Ammonites); 36:9 (Esau father of the Edomites).

5. See, e.g., Gen 18:16 (Sarah, mother of nations); Gen 24:67 (Sarah, mother of Isaac); Gen 27:13–14; 28:2, 7; 29:10 (Rebekah, mother of Jacob). See also Gen 29:31—30:29, naming the four mothers of Jacob's sons, viz: Leah, Bilhah, Zilpah, and Rachel.

6. Gen 16:1–2. In these texts, Sarah is still named Sarai, and Abraham, Abram. Sarah did not merely offer Hagar to Abraham as surrogate in order to bear a child, she *told* him to so act, "that *I* shall obtain children by her." Emphasis supplied. Compare Steinberg's more literal translation: "that I will be built up by it." Steinberg, *Kinship and Marriage*, 62. Steinberg gives a detailed analysis of the Sarah-Abraham-Hagar cycle of stories, ibid., 61–65, 77–81.

7. Gen 16:6.

8. Isaac is mentioned here by name in ancient Greek versions and the Vulgate, but not in the Hebrew text.

of this slave woman shall not be heir with my son Isaac" (Gen 21:10).[9] Again, Abraham did as he was told, even though "the thing was very displeasing" to him.[10]

There being no formal marriage ceremonies in those days, Hagar may or may not have been Abraham's wife. Sarah thought she was beginning to act too much like one. Hagar was a remarkably determined and competent person. It is unclear whether she bore her (and Abraham's) son, Ishmael, while still in the wilderness, or after she had returned to Abraham's camp (Gen 16:7–15). In any case, Hagar again managed to survive the hardships of life in the wilderness, along with her son, after Abraham, once more, at Sarah's command, cast her out (Gen 21:8–21).

Rebekah, who was to become Isaac's wife and the mother of Jacob and Esau, is likewise presented as a determined and autonomous personality. Although Laban, Rebekah's brother, proposes to let Abraham's servant "take her" to Abraham as wife for his son, Isaac, the decision whether she would actually go is left to Rebekah herself. Following preliminary colloquies, Laban and his (and Rebekah's) mother call Rebekah and ask her, "Will you go with this man?" To which she replied, "I will go."[11]

After her sons Jacob and Esau come of age, and Isaac has "grown old and his eyes were dim so that he could not see" (Gen 27:1), Rebekah arranges a deception whereby her husband, Isaac, is tricked into giving his

---

9. Compare Exum, "Mother in Israel," 75–78. Exum characterizes the situation as follows: "Both Sarah and Hagar are victims of a patriarchal society that stresses the importance of sons and of a narrative structure that revolves around the promise of a son. Sadly, but not surprisingly in such a context, they make victims of each other." Ibid., 77. See Frymer-Kensky, *Reading Women*, 225–37 regarding the complexities of the Hagar-Sarai relationship.

10. Gen 21:11. God then tells Abraham, "Whatever Sarah says to you, do as she tells you," reassuring him that both sons will have important descendants (Gen 21:12–13). See Steinberg, *Kinship and Marriage*, 78 n.92, commenting on Sarah's demands in Genesis 16 and 21: "[B]oth episodes present a situation where the wife gets her way." As to Sarah's dominance, vis-á-vis Abraham, see Starr, *Bible Status*, 60–65. "The translators of 1 Peter iii:6 represent Sarah as an obedient wife, subservient to the will of her lord, but the reader will notice that in the Old Testament narrative, on every occasion where there was a clash of wills, it was Abraham, and not [Sarah], who yielded." Ibid., 64.

11. Gen 24:57–58. See also Gen 24:5, 8, and 39, which anticipate that "the woman" would be free to decide whether or not to go with the servant and become Isaac's wife. So also Ebeling, *Women's Lives*, 84. As to Rebekah's character, see Starr, *Bible Status*, 70: "She went to Canaan and became the wife of Isaac, and subsequent events proved that she, like Sarah, was quite equal to the task of managing her husband."

blessing to Jacob—her favorite son—instead of to Esau[12] (whose Hittite wives she cannot abide),[13] the son Isaac had intended to bless. Just as Sarah determined which of her husband's sons would be his (and her) heir, her daughter-in-law, Rebekah, chose which of her own and Isaac's sons would receive his blessing.[14] Rebekah then tells Isaac that she is totally opposed to Jacob marrying any of the local women, and so Isaac dutifully sends Jacob back to Paddam-Aram, with instructions to marry one of *her* nieces.

There, Jacob becomes infatuated with Rachel, one of Laban's daughters.[15] Sly uncle Laban then arranges for Jacob to marry Leah, his other daughter, instead; all the while—until morning light reveals otherwise—Jacob believed he was marrying Rachel.[16] Necessarily, both Rachel and Leah were Laban's accomplices, if not co-conspirators, in perpetrating this fraud upon their prospective husband. As the result, Jacob ended up having to agree to work a total of fourteen years for his uncle Laban.[17] A few years later, after her sister, Leah, had borne several sons, Rachel addressed Jacob in strong language, blaming him for the fact that she had not yet borne any children: "When Rachel saw that she bore Jacob no children, she envied her sister; and she said to Jacob, 'Give me children, or I shall die!'" (Gen 30:1) Jacob's unsympathetic answer was that God had "withheld" from her "the fruit of the womb." In response, and to resolve the impasse, Rachel then took the initiative and *told* Jacob to have intercourse with her maid, Bilhah: "Go into her, [so] that she may bear upon my knees, and even I may have children through her" (Gen

12. Gen 27:5–38.

13. Gen 27:46.

14. The blessing, evidently, was understood to bestow tangible as well as intangible benefits on its recipient.

15. See Gen 29:1–12. Jacob also, evidently, was impressed with Rachel's family's wealth: Gen 29:9–10.

16. Gen 29:15–26. Some interpreters have suggested that Laban's reference to "wages" in Gen 29:15 meant that his daughter, Rachel, was regarded as "property." Jacob, who "loved" Rachel, and wished to marry her, proposed that, instead of being paid wages, he was willing to serve Laban for seven years "for [his] younger daughter Rachel." The narrator does not represent Rachel as "wages" or "property."

17. Gen 29:15–30. The fact that Jacob had wanted and intended to marry Rachel, rather than Leah, may well have contributed to Leah's sense of being unwanted or even hated, and prompted her attempt to gain Jacob's affection by bearing him a greater number of sons (Gen 29–30). Compare Exum, "Mother in Israel" and Scholz, *Women's Hebrew Bible*, quoted below, note 19.

30:3).[18] Jacob was to do so, in order that *Rachel* would have children.[19] Later, Jacob again dutifully obeyed his wife, this time, Leah, when she told him to have intercourse with her yet again (Gen 30:16). It may be noted that when Jacob's sons were born, Leah and Rachel were the ones who gave them their names.[20]

Rachel was not altogether subservient to her father, either.[21] In due course, Jacob stealthily undertook to get away from Laban. While Jacob was packing up his family and all the property he felt entitled to, Rachel stole her father's *teraphim* or "household gods," which probably were understood not only as having some kind of religious importance but also as providing title to the family property. And, despite her father's demand to give them back, Rachel continued to conceal them.[22] Here, again, Rachel acted on her own initiative, this time in tacit defiance of her father.

Judah, Jacob's and Leah's son, was the "father" for whom the later tribe, and later still, the kingdom of Judah were named.[23] He figures prominently in Genesis 38, where he is remembered for his failure to require his third son, Shelah, to marry Tamar, the widow of his first-born son, Er.[24] Here, again, we see a woman, this time Tamar, wife, then widow of Jacob's grandson, acting boldly to assert her own interests and also to

18. Similarly, as previously mentioned, Sarah had told her husband, Abraham, to have intercourse with her maid, Hagar, so that she, Sarah, might have children by her. As will be noted below, the story of Ruth also involved surrogate parenthood.

19. Compare Exum, "Mother in Israel," 79: "Genesis 29–30 describes a child-bearing contest between the rival sisters through which Israel is built up . . . We are again aware of the androcentric perspective, which values a woman for her ability to produce sons . . ." See also Scholz, *Women's Hebrew Bible*, 83–88, characterizing Gen 29–30 as "an androcentric story par excellence." Ibid., 83.

20. Gen 29:32—30:24. Jacob renamed Rachel's last son, after she died in childbirth. Gen 35:17–18.

21. See also Gen 19:30–38. This is the story about the daughters of Lot, Abraham's nephew, who take advantage of their father so that they might "preserve offspring," by getting him drunk and then lying with him while he was unaware of what was happening. The story explains the origins of the Moabites and Ammonites and recognizes them as somewhat disreputable relations of Abraham's descendants. See Steinberg, *Kinship and Marriage*, 70–76.

22. Gen 31:30–35. Rachel hid these "gods" under her camel saddle and "sat upon them"—no doubt a mark of disrespect for these purported deities.

23. The terms "Jew" and "Judaism" also derive from this name.

24. See below, chapter 8, as to the story of Judah and Tamar, also discussing levirate marriage.

secure the succession of Abraham's descendants that would later culminate in the births of David and a series of subsequent kings of Judah.[25] She did so at great risk to herself, but also adroitly arranged to obtain evidence that would vindicate her at the critical moment.[26] She did not simply defer to her father-in-law or accept his failure to act responsibly. It is said that Judah "did not lie with her again" (Gen 38:26), but it may be assumed that they were considered to be married. The story represents another, perhaps common law, version of levirate marriage.[27]

Notwithstanding the ancient story about the Garden of Eden, in which YHWH/God tells the woman that her husband "shall rule over" her (Gen 3:16), none of the so-called "patriarchs" is depicted ruling over his wife.[28] Moreover, as has been mentioned, none of the stories about the so-called "patriarchs" in Genesis ever even characterizes any of these men as a "patriarch." Nor do later biblical narratives provide any instances of husbands ruling over their wives.

25. And eventually, as Matthew's Gospel tells the story, of Joseph, husband of Mary, the mother of Jesus (Matt 1:1–16).

26. See Levine, "Legal Themes," 104: "Tamar was a woman who took bold initiatives on her own behalf, which resulted in preserving the family line of Judah when it was threatened with extinction. Her acts were a risk to her own life and compromised her father-in-law, but they achieved the effective goal of the levirate, through a substitution."

27. As to levirate marriage, see below, chapters 5, 6, and 8.

28. See Starr's summary of relations between the "patriarchs" and their wives: "In closing our study of the status of women in the patriarchal age we note this fact: in no recorded incident, in no passage of Scripture, is the subordination of woman taught or even implied during this period . . . The freedom and independence of the married woman in the patriarchal period puts to shame much of modern jurisprudence. Her property rights were assured to a degree scarcely equaled by our most advanced legislation." *Bible Status*, 71. And, more recently, Ebeling, *Women's Lives*, 28: "[T]here are problems applying the patriarchal model to ancient Israel, and passages in the Hebrew Bible attest to the primary roles of women in important family decisions and customs, such as marriage." See also ibid., 147: "My study questions the perception that Israelite women were 'submissive chattel in an oppressive patriarchy.'" See also Susanne Scholz, *Women's Hebrew Bible*, 62–65, discussing the nuanced proposals by Carol L. Meyers and Silvia Schroer as to the place of women in early Israel and subsequent exilic and postexilic society.

2

Other Stories about Biblical
Husbands and Wives

Bathsheba develops into a player, acting to become the queen
mother and have her son enthroned as the heir.

— Tikva Frymer-Kensky

SUBSEQUENT BIBLICAL NARRATIVES RARELY touch upon relations
between husbands and wives. The few that do, likewise, present the
wives as resourceful, independent, and often powerful figures, hardly
kowtowing to their mates. To be considered here are accounts concerning
David and three women who became his wives; Jezebel and her husband,
King Ahab of Israel; and Anna and her husband, Tobit.[1] Texts commenting generally on relations between wives and husbands are considered
below in chapter 5.

Three wives figure as strong personalities in biblical stories about
David. The earliest of these concerns Abigail, initially, the wife of one
Nabal.[2] David has escaped from Saul, and is now trying to feed his own
rebel army of several hundred men. He sends ten "young men" to Nabal, a
man of great wealth with instructions to offer to "protect" Nabal's people
and his sheep in exchange for an unspecified, but no doubt sizeable "gift."[3]

---

1. The story about Vashti, another case in point, is considered below in chapter 4.
An early vignette features Lamech and his wives, Adah and Zillah. In brief, it tells that
these wives bore a daughter and sons who became "fathers" of persons with certain occupations and skills, and that Lamech told Adah and Zillah to listen to his bit of boorish
braggadocio (Gen 4:19–24). It is not said whether they did so.

2. 1 Sam 25:1–42.

3. Here is an early instance of what in modern times came to be called "the protection
racket." Compare Frymer-Kensky, Reading Women, 316: "David . . . has in fact brought

Nabal fails to recognize his peril and rudely rejects their proposition;[4] but his wise (and beautiful) wife, Abigail, hearing what has happened, promptly sizes up the situation and sends David a generous assortment of food supplies.[5] She, herself, hurries to David to apologize for her husband's folly, and ask his forgiveness—lest he take revenge—adding words of praise for David such as to show him great respect.[6] The result is that David changes his mind, grants her petition, and does not massacre Nabal and his people after all. On learning what has happened, Nabal dies of apoplexy, and David then woos and marries Abigail. There can be no doubt that the narrator intended the reader to understand that Abigail was much wiser than Nabal, her husband, when she effectively over-ruled his ill-tempered and ill-considered rejection of David's proposition.

The next vignette is the scene where David, who has just been installed as king of Israel, is celebrating the arrival of the "ark of God" in Jerusalem. His wife, Michal, daughter of Saul (in whose stead David now reigns), "saw King David leaping and dancing before YHWH; and she despised him in her heart" (2 Sam 6:16).[7] And later she tells him so: "How the king of Israel honored himself today, uncovering himself today before the eyes of his servants' maids, as one of the vulgar fellows shamelessly uncovers himself!" (2 Sam 6:20). David replies in terms that do him no credit.[8] Theirs may have become an unhappy marriage, but there is no indication that Michal abased herself before David.

It may be recalled that David married Bathsheba after first forcing her to commit adultery with him, and then arranging for the murder of her husband, Uriah, in order to cover up the earlier offense.[9] The prophet

[good to Nabal] through his protection."

4. "Shall I take my bread and my water and my meat that I have killed for my shearers, and give it to men who come from I do not know where?" (1 Sam 25:11).

5. 1 Sam 25:18–27.

6. 1 Sam 25:24–31. Though indulging in fulsome flattery, she presents a remarkably tactful and effective petition. Compare Frymer-Kensky, "Bible and Women's Studies," 22, referring to Abigail's "brilliant rhetoric."

7. Michal also may have become disenchanted with David because he had forcibly taken her from her husband, Paltiel, who loved her, merely in order to strengthen his case for replacing Saul, her father, as king of Israel (2 Sam 3:12–21).

8. "I will make myself yet more contemptible than this, and I will be abased in your eyes; but by the maids of whom you have spoken, by them I shall be held in honor." 2 Sam 16:22.

9. 2 Sam 11:1–27. Compare Frymer-Kensky, *Reading Women*, 280: "[David] actually commits administrative assassination by arranging Uriah's death."

Nathan condemns David—or prompts him to condemn himself—for murdering Uriah and for taking Uriah's wife, Bathsheba, to be his own wife.[10] Over the course of some long time, David has many sons by his several wives, and after these were born, Bathsheba bears him another son, Solomon. Still more time passes. David is now old, bedridden, and possibly senile.[11] Adonijah, David's oldest surviving son, reasonably expects to succeed his father as king in the near future. But what happens instead is that Bathsheba and the prophet Nathan[12] conspire to take advantage of David's failing memory. They induce him to "recall" that he had promised Bathsheba that her young son, Solomon, would come to the throne after his death.[13] One could imagine that, whatever else may have motivated her, Bathsheba's involvement in arranging for her own son to succeed David as king was a way of getting back at him for sexually assaulting her and killing her husband, Uriah. In any case, like Sarah, who chose which son (her own) would be her husband's heir, and Rebekah, who arranged for her favorite son, Jacob, to receive her husband's blessing, Bathsheba (aided and abetted by Nathan), saw to it that her own son, Solomon, rather than any of David's older sons, became king after he died.[14]

After Solomon died, his son Rehoboam inherited the throne. Unwisely, Rehoboam systematically mistreated the Northern (Israelite) members of the still tenuously united kingdoms of Israel and Judah. Consequently, ca. 922 BCE, the Northerners broke away and re-estab-

10. In the parable or "case" of the rich man, the poor man, and the latter's pet lamb. 2 Sam 12:1–15.

11. 1 Kgs 1:1–4.

12. Nathan may have intended to help give effect to his earlier condemnation of David, where he had warned David that because he had killed Uriah and taken his wife, "[YHWH] will raise up evil against you out of your own house" (2 Sam 12:7–11).

13. See 1 Kgs 1:11–40. Here Nathan tells Bathsheba to go into David's presence with this story, and while she was "still speaking" he would come in and "confirm" her words. See also Frymer-Kensky, *Reading Women*, 280: "Bathsheba develops into a player, acting to become the queen mother and have her son enthroned as the heir." Later traditions try to legitimate these proceedings by indicating that it all happened according to divine plan. See, e.g., 1 Chr 22:6—23:1; 28:5—29:28. Chronicles does not include any mention of the David-Bathsheba-Uriah events, or the Nathan-Bathsheba coup d'état. Compare Ebeling, *Women's Lives*, 82, describing the episode as an instance "of women counseling their husbands behind the scenes."

14. So also Frymer-Kensky, *Reading Women*, 280: "Bathsheba determines the destiny of Solomon in the grand manner of Sarah and Rivka [Rebekah]."

lished the separate kingdom of Israel, which afterwards was ruled by a turbulent succession of dynasties and kings.

One of those Northern kings, Ahab, wanted very much to acquire the vineyard belonging to a neighbor named Naboth.[15] But Naboth did not wish to sell his ancestral property or even trade it for a better vineyard. Ahab, though king, was a somewhat limited monarch, and so went home, "vexed and sullen," lay down on his bed with his face to the wall and stopped eating. His Phoenician-born wife Jezebel, however, was not bound by Israelite scruples, and promptly had Naboth "set up" or "framed" by a pair of "scoundrels"[16] who charged him with treason, a capital offense.[17] Biblical tradition also credits Jezebel with sponsoring four hundred and fifty prophets of Ba'al and four hundred prophets of Asherah (1 Kgs 18:19), terrorizing the prophet Elijah because he had mocked and defeated the Ba'al prophets and ordered them all slaughtered (1 Kgs 18:20—19:3), and generally speaking, with inciting Ahab to do evil.[18] Jezebel may not have been a nice person, but she was a powerful one; as powerful as her husband, the king.

The Bible contains yet another husband-wife sketch. This is found in the Old Testament Apocrypha, in the story of Tobit and Anna, which probably was written toward the end of the biblical period.[19] Tobit has remembered that Gabael, a relative living some distance away, owes him money. He decides to send his son, Tobias, to collect it. Tobit's wife, Anna, who is introduced early in the story—another strong and independent personality—is unimpressed with her husband's purported righteousness. According to Tobit:

> [M]y wife Anna earned money at women's work. She used to send the product to the owners. Once when they paid her wages, they also gave her a kid; and when she returned to me it began to bleat. So I said to her, "Where did you get the kid? It is not stolen, is it? Return it to the owners; for it is not right to eat what is stolen." And

15. See 1 Kgs 21:1–4.

16. 1 Kgs 21:10, 13 (NRSV).

17. 1 Kgs 21:5–16. Under ancient Near Eastern common law, property of a person convicted of treason would pass to the state, not to the person's heirs. See Westbrook, *Property and Family*, 123–24.

18. See 1 Kgs 21:25: "There was none who sold himself to do what was evil in the sight of YHWH like Ahab, whom Jezebel his wife incited."

19. For a fuller account, see Hiers, *Trinity Guide* 154–56.

she said, "It was given to me as a gift in addition to my wages." But
I did not believe her, and told her to return it to the owners; and I
blushed for her. Then she replied to me, "Where are your charities
and your righteous deeds? You seem to know everything!" (Tob
2:11–14)

Anna is not happy about sending Tobias after the money, and tells
her husband why: "Why have you sent our child away? Is he not the staff
of our hands as he goes in and out before us? Do not add money to money,
but consider it rubbish as compared to our child? For the life that is given
to us by the Lord is enough for us" (Tob 5:17–18).

The journey took longer than expected, Tobias and his traveling
companion have not yet returned, and the parents are worried—though
for different reasons—and take the occasion to have a good family row:

Now his father Tobit was counting each day, and when the days
for the journey had expired and they did not arrive, he said, "Is it
possible that he has been detained? Or is it possible that Gabael
had died and there is no one to give him the money?" And he was
greatly distressed. And his wife said to him, "The lad has perished;
his long delay proves it." Then she began to mourn for him, and
said, "Am I not distressed, my child, that I let you go, you who are
the light of my eyes?" But Tobit said to her, "Be still and stop wor-
rying; he is well." And she answered him, "[You] be still and stop
deceiving me; my child has perished." (Tob 10:1–7)

Husband and wife have their own concerns, and each asks (or tells) the
other to "shut up." Neither appears particularly deferential to the other.

From this survey, it can be concluded that biblical wives neither
felt, nor were depicted as subordinate or subservient to their husbands.[20]

20. A few other accounts might be mentioned. For instance: the story about Job's wife
who, early in that narrative, bluntly advises (or tells) him to end his misery and get it over
with: "Do you still hold fast to your integrity? Curse God and die" (Job 2:9). And also, of
course, the story of the first man, the first woman, and the forbidden fruit in the Garden
of Eden. Here, the woman considers three good reasons to eat, does so, and hands some
to her husband, who immediately follows her example, without pausing for reflection,
let alone any Miltonian agonizing re-appraisal (Gen 3:6). See Trible, *God and Rhetoric*,
113; and, same author, "Eve and Miriam," 11–15 (identifying the woman as the leading
partner in the Garden scene).

The case of Hosea and his wife (and/or concubine) is more complicated. Whether
Hosea's wife, Gomer (Hos 1), is the same person as the slave-concubine he purchased
in chapter 3, cannot be determined. Nor can it be determined whether Hosea knew of
this woman's or these women's harlotrous or adulterous histories and proclivities before

Several other biblical women, whether married or single, were remembered for their accomplishments and status in their respective communities. It may be noticed that none of them was submissive, either. Their stories are considered in the next two chapters.

---

marrying (or purchasing) her or them. If he did, it would have been to dramatize his message, as did the prophets Isaiah and Ezekiel. (For example, Isa 8:1–4; Ezek 12:1–16). If he did not, it is noteworthy that he did not charge her (or them) with adultery, a capital offense. In both chapters, the harlotrous and/or adulterous wife or concubine symbolizes Israel's relation with YHWH, and the narrative says little or nothing about Hosea's relationship with any actual woman or women. Chapter 2 relates entirely to YHWH's prospective punishment and restoration of Israel, with its eschatological and ecological covenant and finale in Hos 2:18–23, and tells nothing about interactions between Hosea and the woman or women he may have married. Neither chapter appears to have been intended to prescribe relations between husbands and wives.

3

Other Biblical Women of Recognized Status or Importance

> Unlike Shakespeare's Lady Macbeth, Ja'el did not need to induce her husband to assassinate their unsuspecting guest; she did it all herself.

TWO RELATIVELY UNSUNG HEROINES may be mentioned first: Shiphrah and Puah. They were the two midwives who continued to deliver Hebrew women's baby sons, in defiance of Pharaoh's orders to kill them at birth (Exod 1:15–21). Doing so called not only for courage, but also for remarkable enterprise, considering that the land of Egypt had become "filled" with the descendants of Israel (Exod 1:7). It might be said that the survival of the people of Israel was due in large part to the brave and devoted efforts of Shiphrah and Puah.[1]

Women play critical roles in the course of events that resulted in Moses' being spared Pharaoh's subsequent order calling for drowning all newborn Hebrew male infants in the Nile. Moses' mother, Jochebed,[2] first hides her new baby then places him in a basket or "ark" out of view. Moses' sister, Miriam, stands by. Pharaoh's daughter finds the baby and has "pity on him." Miriam asks the daughter, "Shall I go and call you a nurse from the Hebrew women to nurse the child for you?" She does, and Pharaoh's daughter adopts the child, who then lives to play his major roles in the emergence of Israel as a nation.[3]

---

1. See Starr, *Bible Status*, 156; Exum, "Mother in Israel," 80–81.

2. So named later in Exod 6:20.

3. Exod 2:1–10. See Exum, "Mother in Israel," 80–81, reviewing the episode, noting many ironic touches, Exum also points out that later, Moses' life was again saved by a woman, this time, by his wife, Zipporah (Exod 4:24–26).

15

Five women are remembered for important deeds reported in the books of Joshua and Judges: Rahab, Deborah, Ja'el, the "certain woman" who killed the tyrant, Abimelech, and the Philistine heroine, Delilah. Rahab, the Canaanite prostitute, facilitated the Israelites' conquest of Jericho. First she hid the two Israelite men whom Joshua had set to spy out the land of Canaan which the Israelites planned to enter after their long years of wandering in the Sinai Peninsula. Rahab then helped the spies escape, letting them down by a rope from the window of her house which was built into one of the city's walls. The spies eventually reported back to Joshua, who then proceeded to direct Israel's triumph over Jericho.[4]

Perhaps the most notable among these great and famous women was Deborah. The book of Judges characterizes Deborah as both a prophet or "prophetess"[5] and a judge (Judg 4:4). Of all the judges of Israel, she alone is portrayed as acting in a judicial capacity: "She used to sit under the palm of Deborah between Ramah and Bethel in the hill country of Ephraim; and the people of Israel came up to her for judgment" (Judg 4:5). She is also represented as, in effect, commander-in-chief, commissioning a man named Barak, to lead the Israelites' army against the Canaanites. Barak did so, acting under orders relayed from YHWH through Deborah. Barak was so impressed with Deborah's importance that he insisted on her going into battle with him; she did, and, in the face of opposing forces, urged him on.[6] Barak's people defeated the Canaanite army. Deborah also is credited with composing and singing—along with Barak—a "song" commemorating this great victory.[7] Deborah is one of just three judges who were said to have established eras of lasting peace or "rest": After her reign, the narrator says, "the land had rest for forty years" (Judg 5:31c).

---

4. Josh 2:1–24. For these good deeds, Rahab and her family were spared when Jericho was destroyed (Josh 6:1–25). Compare Scholz, *Women's Hebrew Bible*, 119–20 (viewing Rahab as "a problematic figure" from "a postcolonial feminist perspective" because she "is co-opted into the colonizing project"). Compare Frymer-Kensky, *Reading Women*, 34–42 (portraying Rahab positively, e.g., as "the 'midwife' of the embryonic Israel," and "the first of the female oracles who appear throughout the historical books," ibid., 36, 37). See also ibid., 297–98.

5. The term "prophetess" is used here and in texts following the RSV translations. Alternative translations are "prophet," and "female prophet."

6. "And Deborah said to Barak, 'Up! For this is the day in which YHWH has given Sisera into your hand.'" Judg 4:14.

7. Judg 5:1–31. This "song" is considered one of, if not the oldest unit of ancient Israelite literature. As to Deborah and her "song," see the careful and appreciative commentary by Starr, *Bible Status*, 140–44.

Another important woman, Ja'el, also is remembered in connection with this victory. Sisera was commander of the Canaanite forces. After his army was defeated, Sisera fled to the home (tent) of Ja'el, the wife of a man named Heber. Ja'el invited Sisera into their tent, offered him milk to drink, and then murdered him.[8]

The unnamed "certain woman" who fatally injured Abimelech, the ruthless king of Israel, by dropping a millstone stone on his head while he and his men were laying siege to the city of Thebez (Judg 9:50–57) also deserves mention here. Her deed put an end to his cruel rule. Another unnamed, but important woman, acted critically in a somewhat later time. This was the "wise woman" whose initiative put a stop to one of the murderous civil wars that plagued Israel during the time of David. She did so by arranging to have the decapitated head of Sheba, the son of Bichri[9] (the opposing forces' leader), "thrown" down "over the wall" of the besieged city to Joab, David's commanding general (2 Sam 20:14–22).[10] These were formidable women.[11]

One other heroine whose deeds are remembered in the book of Judges is Delilah. To be sure, she was a heroine only from the standpoint of Israel's dominant neighbors, the Philistines. As the story is told, Samson, a physically powerful but morally and perhaps mentally challenged Israelite, had been engaging in eco-terrorism and other ill-considered acts of violence against the Philistines (Judg 14:19—15:8). The Philistines decided that Samson had to be dealt with, so they asked Delilah, a young Philistine woman whom Samson "loved," to entice him and find out the secret source of his great strength. She did so through a series of ruses, with the result that the Philistines were able to subdue him

8. In the prose account, she gives him milk to drink, covers him, and then, after he falls asleep, takes a hammer and drives a tent peg through his head (Judg 4:17–22). In the poetic Song, Ja'el brings Sisera milk curds in "a lordly bowl" and, it seems, kills him while he is standing there drinking from the bowl (Judg 5:24–27). According to Judg 4:17, there had been peace between the Canaanites and her husband's family. Unlike Shakespeare's Lady Macbeth, Ja'el did not need to induce her husband to assassinate their unsuspecting guest; she did it all herself. Compare Frymer-Kensky, *Reading Women*, 335: "Yael . . . is the archetype of those who conquer their powerful adversaries by faith and determination."

9. This Sheba was a Benjaminite, as had been Saul, the King of Israel whose throne David now claimed. Both Absalom and Sheba had tried to rally Israelite nationalism against David's rule.

10. See Frymer-Kensky, *Reading Women*, 61.

11 See also the story of Judith, considered below in chapter 4.

(Judg 16:4–21). Whatever the historical basis of the story may have been, it is noteworthy that the biblical account fully credits Delilah for her cleverness and persistence in aiding her fellow countrymen and women—not withstanding their being Philistines.

Like Deborah, a few other biblical women also were considered prophets. Foremost among these, perhaps, was Miriam, Moses' and Aaron's sister, who is identified as "the prophetess" in Exodus 15:20. Moreover, like Deborah, Miriam sang—having presumably composed it—a famous "song," the Song of Miriam, which, like the Song of Deborah, is considered one of the oldest fragments of ancient biblical literature:

> Sing to YHWH, for he has triumphed gloriously;
> the horse and his rider he has thrown into the sea.[12] (Exod 15:21)

Isaiah refers to another woman as "the prophetess," meaning, perhaps, his wife: "And I went to the prophetess, and she conceived and bore a son. Then YHWH said to me, 'Call his name Mahershalalhashbaz . . .'" (Isa 8:3). It is not clear whether this prophetess was recognized as a prophet in her own right.

Another female prophet ("prophetess") played a major role during the period of the Deuteronomic reform. This was Huldah, whose words of judgment and hope were addressed to King Josiah[13] after he had heard a reading from the newly discovered "book of the law." Huldah's words of warning and encouragement (2 Kgs 22:15–20) evidently prompted Josiah to proceed with implementing this important reform (2 Kgs 23:1–25).[14] Some two hundred years later, Nehemiah makes passing reference to "the prophetess Noadiah," one of the prophets who, it seems, attempted (unsuccessfully) to frighten and thus discourage him from rebuilding the walls of Jerusalem.[15] Though relatively few female proph-

---

12. The longer "Song of Moses," found at Exod 15:1–18, may have borrowed from the Song of Miriam. The first stanza of each is nearly identical. As to the importance of Miriam and her Song, see Trible, "Eve and Miriam," 15–24 (arguing brilliantly on the basis of several biblical "fragments" that Miriam figured much more prominently in earlier accounts than in the present, redacted text of Exodus). See also Fiorenza, "Interpreting Patriarchal Traditions," 49–52.

13. 2 Kgs 22:11–14. The account here is repeated with minor variations in 2 Chr 34:22–28.

14. See Frymer-Kensky, *Reading Women*, 324–30, an excellent and appreciative account of Huldah.

15. See Neh 6:1–19. The prophetess Noadiah is mentioned at Neh 6:14. See also Luke 2:36–38, concerning the "prophetess Anna."

ets are named in biblical tradition, according to the prophet Joel, both the sons and daughters of the people of Israel would prophesy in the coming or messianic age.[16]

Two women were recognized as having royal status. They were, in effect, queens of Israel and of Judah. As has been seen, even during her husband's lifetime while he ruled as king over the northern kingdom, Israel, Jezebel was a particularly potent person. Biblical tradition is somewhat sketchy, but it appears that Jezebel functioned as power behind the throne, if not formally as Queen of Israel, following the death of King Ahab and during the reigns of their two sons, Ahaziah and Joram.[17] Athaliah—a granddaughter of King Omri of Israel and possibly a daughter of Ahab,[18] his son—married Jehoram, king of Judah. After Jehoram's death, and that of their son, Ahaziah,[19] Athaliah reigned as Queen over Judah in her own right, during those troubled times.[20] Like Jezebel, her contemporary, Athaliah was assassinated by would-be successors to the throne. She had previously "destroyed [nearly] all the royal family" in order to secure her own place there.

Another woman played a major role in preserving the royal family. Jehosheba, daughter of King Joram (Jehoram), hid her half-brother, Joash, in order to spare him from Athaliah's genocidal purge (2 Kgs 11). Joash (Jehoash) later became king of Judah, and as the story is told in 2 Kings 12, "did what was right in the eyes of YHWH" and reigned for forty years.

Some other women may have exercised royal authority as "queen mother," or the power behind the thrones of their sons: Maacah, Hamutal,

16. Joel 2:28.

17. See 1 Kgs 22:51–53 and 2 Kgs 9:1–37.

18. Her father is not identified. However, according to 2 Kgs 10:1, Ahab had seventy sons. Presumably he also had many daughters, and Athaliah may well have been one of them.

19. See 2 Kgs 8:25–27. The ruling houses of Israel and Judah were inter-related; and the picture is further confused by the fact that each kingdom was ruled in the late ninth century B.C.E. by kings with identical or similar names, viz. Ahaziah, Jehoram (also known as Joram), and Jehoash (also known as Joash).

20. See 2 Kgs 11:1–16. As to Athaliah, see Frymer-Kensky, *Reading Women*, 8–38, and Starr, *Bible Status*, 159. Starr also points out that a highly regarded woman reigned as Queen of the Jewish nation during the Maccabean Period: namely, Alexandra, also known as Salome (139–67 BCE). Ibid., 159–60. As will be mentioned in the following chapter, two women, Vashti and Esther, enjoyed the somewhat honorific title of "queen" as wives of the Persian king, Ahasuerus.

and Nehushta, mothers, respectively, of Kings Asa, Jehoiahaz, and Jehoiachin.[21] Bathsheba probably had done so already during the early years of Solomon's reign.

Two other women with recognized status figure prominently, though in unusual ways. One was the "witch" or medium at Endor, whom Saul consulted on the eve of his final battle with the Philistines. At Saul's request, she "brought up" the spirit of Samuel, whose message of doom understandably terrified Saul. The woman insisted on feeding Saul a nourishing meal to strengthen him for the coming ordeal (1 Sam 28:3–25). Had Saul prevailed against the Philistines, much of the credit would have gone to this woman.

The other was another queen, the Queen of Sheba. The story is told in 1 Kings 10:1–13, to illustrate Solomon's wisdom and wealth. The Queen presents Solomon with a super-abundance of valuable gifts; in return, "King Solomon gave to the Queen of Sheba all that she desired, whatever she asked, besides what was given to her by the bounty of King Solomon" (1 Kgs 10:13). It appears that the Queen may have come out ahead of Solomon in this exchange of opulent gifts.

Perhaps the most highly praised of all biblical women was the mother of the seven martyrs, whose story is told in 4 Maccabees.[22] The final five chapters of that book—and also, co-incidentally, of the edition of the Bible[23] quoted in this book—characterize her in superlative terms. Passing over the account of the martyrs, her sons, it may be enough here to repeat only two verses by way of illustration: "O mother of the nation, vindicator of the law and champion of religion, who carried away the prize of the contest in your heart! O more noble than males in steadfastness, and more manly than men in endurance!" (4 Macc 15:29–30). This encomium despite the fact that the same text refers casually to mothers as "the weaker sex" (4 Macc 15:5). Thus this mother's achievement was

21. See Frymer-Kensky, "Bible and Women's Studies," 23.

22. Fourth Maccabees is included in both the *NOAB-RSV* and *NOAB-NRSV* versions of the OT Apocrypha. However, it is not part of the scripture of any modern religious community. It was included in some versions of the Septuagint (ca. 200 BCE–100 CE), and so was considered part of scripture by many Jews and Christians in early times.

23. See above, Preface, discussing "Old Testament or Hebrew Scriptures." On the other hand, the *NOAB-NRSV* concludes with the New Testament, thus with the Book of Revelation. The Hebrew (Jewish) Bible or *Tanakh*, ends with the *Kethuvim* or "writings," the last of which are 1 and 2 Chronicles. The Old Testament ends with the "Book of the Twelve" prophets, the last of which is Malachi.

considered all the more outstanding. She was also said to have been "an elder" (4 Macc 16:14). The expression "the weaker sex" also is to be found in the New Testament.[24] Women are never so characterized in the Old Testament.

Several more women who were remembered for their important deeds or other merits are considered in the chapter that follows. These include, among others, Ruth, Vashti, Esther, Judith, and Susanna.

24. 1 Pet 3:7: "Likewise you husbands, live considerately with your wives, bestowing honor on the woman as the weaker sex, since you are joint heirs of the grace of life . . ."

4

Women in Books of the Bible
Named for Women

"The command of Queen Esther fixed these practices of Purim, and it was recorded in writing" (Esth 9:32). Esther here steps into Moses' shoes as biblical law-giver.

A FEW WOMEN ARE honored by having biblical books named for them: namely, the Book of Ruth, the Book of Esther, and in the Old Testament Apocrypha, the Book of Judith, and the Story of Susanna.[1] These writings commemorate women for a variety of reasons. Many other biblical writings also focus on women and record their words. In addition to the numerous times women are quoted throughout the Bible, several important texts are also attributed to women: the "Songs" of Deborah, Miriam, and Judith; Hannah's psalm or song (1 Sam 2:1–10); Abigail's petition to David (1 Sam 25:2–31); the prophet Huldah's message to King Josiah (2 Kgs 22:15–20; "the words of Lemuel . . . which his mother taught him" (Prov 31); various declarations or exclamations in the Song of Solomon;[2] and Queen Esther's prayer (Add Esth 14:3–19).

Ruth and Naomi are prominent figures in the "book" named for the former. Both are strong and determined personalities. Ruth is remembered especially for her devotion to her mother-in-law, Naomi, which devotion is epitomized in her much-quoted declaration: "Entreat me not to leave you or to return from following you; for where you go I will go,

---

1. While observing that "Susanna" is part of the "Additions to Daniel" found in the Septuagint and other ancient versions, many modern editions of the Bible present "Susanna" as a separate book. See, e.g., *NOAB-RSV*, Apocrypha section, 213; and *NOAB-NRSV*, Apocrypha, 194.

2. See Kent, "His Desire."

and where you lodge I will lodge; your people shall be my people, and your God my God; where you die I will die, and there will I be buried. May YHWH do so to me and more also if even death parts me from you" (Ruth 1:16–17).

Ruth is also remembered in biblical tradition for carrying out Naomi's instructions by proposing to and marrying Boaz,[3] by whom she had a son who is hailed as *Naomi's* "next of kin": "Then the women said to Naomi, 'Blessed be YHWH, who has not left you this day without next of kin; . . . He shall be to you a restorer of life and a nourisher of your old age, for your daughter-in-law who loves you, who is more to you than seven sons, has borne him'" (Ruth 4:14–15). In effect, Ruth served as surrogate mother on behalf of Naomi, and blessed her with the child who would be her—that is, Naomi's—*go'el* or redeemer.[4] This son was also to be grandfather of David. Ruth's prominence is all the more remarkable in that she was a Moabite, not an Israelite or Judahite.

Two women also play central roles in the book of Esther. One is Queen Vashti, the wife, it seems,[5] of the Persian king (or emperor) Ahasuerus. The other, for whom the book is named, is Esther. Vashti is first in order of appearances.

As the story is told, on the last day of a seven-day banquet, while Ahasuerus' "heart" was "merry with wine," he ordered the royal eunuchs "to bring Queen Vashti before the king, . . . in order to show the peoples and the princes her beauty, for she was fair to behold" (Esth 1:10–11). However, for reasons not stated, "Queen Vashti refused to come at the king's command" (Esth 1:12). Very likely it was understood that she did not care to entertain the king's male, sexist (and probably inebriated)

---

3. See Ruth 3:1–18. The story of Naomi and Ruth and several related legal issues are further considered below in chapters 9 and 11.

4. See Hiers, *Justice and Compassion*, 201–2. See also Trible, "Bible in Transit," 31–33, summarizing recent interpretations of Ruth: "Redemptive, destructive, ambiguous: judgments about the Book of Ruth range from the benign to the fractious. Some of them stay close to the text; some select from it; some stray from it. Far from unique, what happens with this one book extends to readings of countless biblical texts, as feminists flee the land of patriarchy to confront the terrors, blessings, and uncertainties of scripture in the wilderness." Ibid., 33.

The task of interpretation (or hermeneutics), which in the first instance, is to try to uncover the original meaning or intent of a biblical text, is often complicated by an understandable tendency to read it in the light of one's own hopes, fears, concerns, or agendas, in rather the same way one might interpret a Rorschach ink blot design.

5. See references to other "husbands" in Esth 1:17, 20, quoted below.

guests by displaying her body before them. At any rate, her refusal to obey the king's command precipitated a major crisis in the land. The king asked his wise men what to do. One of them, whose name was Memucan, summed up the situation and advised the king as follows:

> "Not only to the king has Queen Vashti done wrong, but also to all the princes and all the peoples who are in all the provinces of King Ahasuerus. For this deed of the queen will be made known to all women, causing them to look with contempt upon their husbands, since they will say, 'King Ahasuerus commanded Queen Vashti to be brought before him, and she did not come.' This very day the ladies of Persia and Media who have heard of the queen's behavior will be telling it to all the king's princes, and there will be contempt and wrath in plenty. If it please the king, let a royal order go forth from him, and let it be written among the laws of the Persians and the Medes so that it may not be altered, that Vashti is to come no more before King Ahasuerus; and let the king give her royal position to another who is better than she. So when the decree made by the king is proclaimed throughout all his kingdom, vast as it is, women will give honor to their husbands, high and low." This advice pleased the king and the princes, and the king did as Memucan proposed; he sent letters to all the royal provinces, to every people in its own language, that every man may be lord in his own house . . . (Esth 1:16–22)

Thus the Persian Empire was spared what might otherwise have been the first women's revolution, and men there could, at least for a while longer, continue to enjoy the idea that their wives honored them. According to this decree, wives throughout the Persian Empire would have to stay in their place—as inferiors and subject to their husbands.[6]

The position of "Queen" (or perhaps number-one harem girl), now being temporarily vacant, a beauty contest was held, and the king selected Esther to succeed Vashti as Queen (Esth 2:2–17). The Old Testament does not report that any beauty contests were ever conducted by Israelites, Judahites, or Jews. Focus in the book now shifts to Esther, herself.

---

6. It should be apparent that this "decree" by King Ahasuerus was not understood as setting the legal or normative standard for marital relations among Israelites or Jews. This was Persian law, not biblical law. No OT law calls on wives to "honor their husbands," or on husbands to be lords in their own houses. Compare texts quoted below in chapter 5, accompanying notes 6 and 37–39.

Esther is remembered not only for her beauty, but also, and especially, for her courage in confronting the Persian King Ahasuerus, who, as the story is told, "reigned from India to Ethiopia over one hundred and twenty-seven provinces" (Esth 1:1). His chief advisor, the despicable Haman, feeling insulted by the Jew Mordecai's refusal to bow and scrape in his presence, plots to destroy all Jews. Earlier, Mordecai had adopted Esther as his daughter. The story moves to its climax as Esther, now King Ahasuerus' "Queen," encouraged by Mordecai, bravely enters the king's presence[7] and tells him about Haman's plot, whereupon the King decides to spare the Jewish people from the terrible fate otherwise in store.[8] The event is commemorated in the festival of Purim.[9] Esther, along with Mordecai, is said to have ordained that Jews in later times must observe this festival (Esth 9:29–31); and Esther alone is so credited in the verse following: "The command of Queen Esther fixed these practices of Purim, and it was recorded in writing" (Esth 9:32). Esther here steps into Moses' shoes as biblical lawgiver.

Judith is a particularly striking figure. As the story unfolds, she shrewdly plans and proceeds to entice and then kill Holofernes, the powerful but malevolent commander of enemy forces bent on destroying the Jewish people. The story culminates with her cutting off his head, and then calling forth the Jewish armies who crushingly defeat these enemies.[10] The book of Judith concludes with her song of thanksgiving, Judith 16:1–17, in the tradition of the songs of Miriam and of Moses. The last sentence of the book is suggestive of some of the final commentaries on judges of Israel in early times: "And no one ever again spread terror among the people of Israel in the days of Judith, or for a long time after her death."[11]

Susanna is remembered for her refusal to commit adultery, even when faced with certain death if she failed to accede to the two wicked

---

7. See Brueggemann, *Disruptive Grace*, 327–28. Esther's bravery is emphasized even more strongly in the Septuagint version, known in the OT Apocrypha as "Additions to the book of Esther." See Add Esth 14–15, particularly the melodramatic account in Add Esth chapter 15.

8. See Esth 1–7.

9. Esth 9:23–32.

10. Jdt 1–15. One thinks of such biblical parallels as Ja'el's killing the unsuspecting Sisera (Judg 4–5), and David's killing, and then beheading Goliath (1 Sam 17).

11. Jdt 16:25. Compare, e.g., Judg 3:30; 5:31c; 8:28.

elders' demand.[12] Even though these elders were also judges, Susanna did not allow either their male or their official status to overcome her own moral convictions. She was not only "a very beautiful woman," but also "one who feared the Lord," having been taught "according to the law of Moses" by her righteous parents.[13] Although she had "cried out with a loud voice" when first confronted by these scheming elders (v. 24), she does not testify at her trial. After she is condemned to die, however, she calls, again with a loud voice, to God, protesting her innocence. When the Lord hears her cry, he calls on Daniel, who proceeds to act as her defense counsel at re-trial, this time exposing the depraved elders' false charge, and completely vindicating Susanna.[14] Susanna is remembered as a model of rectitude, who remained faithful to the law and to her husband.

Like Lappidoth, the husband of Deborah, Heber, the husband of Ja'el, and Shallum, the husband of Huldah, Susanna's husband, Joakim, though named, has no part in the dramatic narrative in which his wife is the central figure. Likewise, Zelophehad is remembered because of his daughters, not the other way around (Num 27:1–11). As has been seen, several other women figure prominently in biblical narratives without any mention of male relatives.[15] These husbands are mentioned only because of their famous wives. Judith's husband, Manasseh, and also her male forebears are named (Jdt 8:1–2), but only because of their association with Judith, the heroine of the book named in her honor.

---

12. Sus vv. 19–23.

13. Ibid., vv. 2–3. This text may, or may not mean that Susanna, herself, had studied the law. Clearly, she knew how that law applied in her own circumstances.

14. As to jurisprudential features of this story, see Hiers, *Justice and Compassion*, 70–72, 139, 141, 142.

15. For instance, Shiprah, Puah, Rahab, and the two unnamed women who took decisive action to save their communities from besieging enemies. See above, chapter 3. Compare Sharp, *Wrestling the Word*, 115: "Women characters in Scripture are few and far between, and the females who are featured in narratives are male-identified; that is, they are narratologically described and defined by their relationships as wives of men, sexual partners of men, daughters of men, or mothers of sons." In biblical society, genealogies were patrilineal: people were named as sons or daughters of their fathers. See detailed study by Steinberg, *Kinship and Marriage*. Likewise, in modern American society, men and women traditionally bear their fathers' names. Even wives who wish to keep their "own" name usually take the name of their fathers' fathers. The fact that biblical genealogies were patrilineal may be one reason fewer women than men are named in OT traditions.

To what extent these stories recall historical personalities and events remains an open question. Even if largely legendary, they nevertheless reflect positive attitudes toward women.[16] It would be surprising if women were so highly regarded, yet not considered persons with legal capacity.

16. Compare Bird, "Images of Women," 60–61: "[T]he roles played by women in [the historical writings] are almost exclusively subordinate and / or supporting roles . . . Only Deborah and Jezebel stand on their own feet—possibly also Miriam and Huldah." Compare Cahill, *Sex, Gender and Christian Ethics*, 143: "[I]mportant women—Sarah, Rebeka, Rachel, Leah, Zipporah, Deborah, Naomi, Ruth, Abigail, and Judith—have major roles to play, at least in the biblical story." Hollyday identifies and discusses some twenty-nine women important in OT narratives. Hollyday, *Clothed with the Sun*, 3–153. The present study identifies fifty women named in OT narratives, along with a dozen more whose names were not recorded, but were remembered for their significant deeds, words, or status.

5

Perspectives on Women
in other Biblical Traditions

Women were not simply property that could be bought and sold,
. . . and nowhere is a man's absolute sovereignty over his wife indicated in the biblical text.

—Jennie R. Ebeling

B IBLICAL TRADITION PRESENTS A wide range of attitudes regarding women. Perspectives on women come to expression in other
stories or narratives, in many legal texts, and in numerous wisdom sayings found in the books of Proverbs and Sirach, the latter also known as
Ecclesiasticus.[1] As will be seen, these perspectives express both extremely
positive appreciation, as well as peculiarly negative attitudes. For present
purposes, it is enough to notice that, either way, women are viewed as
important and powerful figures in biblical times. The texts considered
here first are those that reflect attitudes toward women, generally; and
then, more specifically, those indicating attitudes regarding, respectively,
"loose women," mothers, daughters, wives, and widows.

WOMEN GENERALLY

Most of the few adverse comments about women in Old Testament times
appear in Sirach. For instance, in Sirach 25:24, the sage laments: "From
a woman sin had its beginning, and because of her we all die."[2] And in

1. Also known as The Wisdom of Jesus the Son of Sirach. See Sir 50:27 as to Sirach's
authorship.

2. Actually, in the Genesis account of events in the Garden blame for humankind's
subsequent problematic condition is apportioned evenly among all three participants

the same vein: "Better is the wickedness of a man than a woman who does good; it is a woman who brings shame and disgrace" (Sir 42:14).[3] In similar vein, a biblical commentator blames Solomon's apostasy on his foreign wives: it was *they* who "turned away his heart after other gods" (1 Kgs 11:1–3).

On the other hand, many biblical texts reflect a quite positive appreciation of women. In the P creation story, the first woman is said to have been made—like the first man—in the "image of God."[4] Whatever was meant by "image," it is clear that the woman was understood to share that exalted attribute with the man.[5] To the extent that the man was made, somehow, like God, so was the woman. It may also be significant that biblical tradition acknowledges the wisdom (and prudence) of various female creatures, such as Balaam's she-ass (Num 22:21–33); ants (Prov 6:6–8); and migratory birds (Jer 8:7).

Highly positive appreciation of women and their influence also comes to expression in a relatively late biblical text. This is in the story about King Darius' three bodyguards and their debating contest on the topic "what one thing is strongest" (1 Esd 3:4—4:41). One guard argues

---

involved: the serpent, the woman, and the man. These Sirach texts illustrate misinterpretation of earlier biblical tradition from an androcentric perspective within the pages of the Bible itself. Another example is 1 Pet 3:5–6, misconstruing Gen 18:12. See above, chap 1 note 10. As to Sirach's views regarding women, see Hurley, *Man and Woman*, 59–60. Compare the seventeenth-century dramatist, Thomas Otway's words (in *The Orphan*): "What mighty ills have not been done by Woman? Who was't betrayed the Capitol? A Woman. Who lost Marc Antony the world? A Woman. Who was the cause of a long ten years' war and laid at last old Troy in ashes? Woman. Deceitful, damnable, destructive Woman."

3. See also Sir 42:12–13. Sirach also includes the famous seven chapters in praise of "famous men, and our fathers in their generations" which make no mention of great and famous women or mothers. (Sir 44:1—50:21). The book concludes, however, expressing gratitude for wisdom, understood here, as elsewhere, in biblical wisdom writings, as a female being. Sir 51:13–22. See also Sir 1:1–10, at the beginning of the book. Moreover, as will be seen, Sirach also includes many affirmative statements about women.

4. Gen 1:26–27; 5:1–2; 9:6. See Trible, *Rhetoric of Sexuality*, 72–105, suggesting that in the J creation story, "the man" referred to in Gen. 2:7 is better translated as "the earth creature," since this being did not become male until the first woman was made from his rib. And see Sloane, "And he shall rule," 5–6.

5. See Bird, "Images of Women," 71–73; Cahill, *Between the Sexes*, 45–58; and Evans, *Women in the Bible*, 12–14. The second or "J" creation story, in Gen 2, likewise "points to recognition of the woman's fundamental likeness, mutuality, and equality with the man." Junia Pokrifka, "Patriarchy, Biblical Authority," 283. See also ibid., 282–83.

for wine; the second, for "the king." The following excerpt is typical of the third guard's argument:

> Gentlemen, is not the king great, and are not men many, and is not wine strong? Who then is their master, or who is their lord? Is it not women? Women gave birth to the king and to every people that rules over sea and land. From women they came; and women brought up the very men who plant the vineyards from which comes wine . . . If men gather gold and silver or any other beautiful thing, and then see a woman lovely in appearance and beauty, they let all those things go, and gape at her, and with open mouths stare at her, and all prefer her to gold or silver or any other beautiful thing. A man leaves his own father, who brought him up, and his own country, and cleaves to his wife. With his wife he ends his days, with no thought of his father or his mother or his country. Hence you must realize that women rule over you.[6] (1 Esd 4:14–22)

In its terms, this discourse refers not only to beautiful women, but also to mothers and wives. Such women were to be appreciated and admired.

Other biblical texts also express male appreciation of female beauty. The most dramatic instance, perhaps, is the occasion when Jacob first met his cousin, Rachel: "Now when Jacob saw Rachel . . . , [he] went up and rolled the stone from the well's mouth, and watered the flock of Laban his mother's brother. Then Jacob kissed Rachel, and wept aloud" (Gen 29:10–11). This was an emotional, romantic moment, at least for Jacob. The most famous biblical celebration of female (and male) beauty, of course, is the Song of Songs (or Song of Solomon), where male and female lovers address each other (or nearby witnesses) with equally affirming voices, expressing their mutual admiration, desires and affections, often using sexually explicit imagery.[7]

---

6. Compare 1 Tim 5:14, a NT text, recommending that "younger widows marry, bear children, [and] *rule their households.*" Emphasis supplied. See also Schroer, "Feminist Reconstruction," 150: "Proverbs 31:10–31, describes a woman who rules over a household with servants . . ."

7. See Evans, *Woman in the Bible,* 23–24: "[I]n the Song of Solomon the mutuality of the sexes is clearly affirmed. There is no male dominance, no female subordination, and no stereotyping of either sex. The woman is independent, fully the equal of the man." See also Kent, "His Desire," and Hiers, *Trinity Guide,* 92–93. Sexual desire could also result in sexual exploitation or abuse. Most famously, perhaps, in the case of David's rape of Bathsheba (2 Sam 11:2–4). As to biblical laws dealing with alleged adultery and sexual

A man's love for his wife was not limited to his appreciation of her physical charm. For instance, the Genesis narrator says as to Isaac's and Rebekah's first meeting: "Then Isaac brought her . . . and she became his wife; and he loved her. So Isaac was comforted after his mother's death" (Gen 24:67). Isaac, obviously, had also loved his mother. Another account of a man's love for his wife, mentioned previously, was the occasion when, for political reasons, David had Saul's daughter, Michal, taken from her husband, Paltiel so that he, himself, could make her his wife: "But her husband went with her, weeping after her all the way to Bahurim" (2 Sam 3:14–16). Undoubtedly, many other men in biblical times dearly loved the women in their lives.

But one class of women was to be avoided.

"LOOSE WOMEN"

Not all women are regarded favorably. "Loose women," whether prostitutes or adulteresses, are seen as potent threats to innocent or foolish men, particularly in wisdom writings, which are full of admonitions, such as the following:

> She sits at the door of her house,
> > she takes a seat on the high places of the town,
> calling to those who pass by,
> > who are going straight on their way,
> "Whoever is simple, let him turn in here!"
> > And to him who is without sense she says,
> "Stolen water is sweet,
> > and bread eaten in secret is pleasant."
> But he does not know that the shades are there,
> > that her guests are in the depths of Sheol. (Prov 9:14–18)[8]

Sexually transmitted diseases may not yet have been identified in biblical times, but evidently the sage recognized that intimacy with "loose women" could be unhealthy and even fatal.

A text in Ecclesiastes, sometimes construed as misogynist in nature, likewise seems to warn men about the perils of associating with designing

---

assault, see Hiers, *Justice and Compassion*, 97–99, 103–4. As to other sexual offenses, see ibid., 104–6.

8. See also such texts as Prov 2:16–19; 5:3–23; 6:23–35; 7:4–27; 22:14; 23:26–28; and Sir 9:2–9; 19:2–3; 25:21. See also Sir 23:18–27 on marital infidelity on the part of both husbands and wives.

women: "And I found more bitter than death the woman whose heart is snares and nets, and whose hands are fetters; he who pleases God escapes her, but the sinner is taken by her" (Eccl 7:26).

Men would do well to heed the advice of the sages and stay clear of such women as all these. Other kinds of women, however, were to be honored and cared for; particularly mothers.

MOTHERS

The J creation story explains the name of the first woman, Eve, as meaning that "she was the mother of all living" (Gen 3:20).[9] Whether this explanation was understood to mean that Eve was, somehow, the mother of all later and contemporary humans, or, more inclusively, somehow the mother of all living things, it is clear that these are words of high praise. As the primordial ancestress, she was understood to have had, and to continue to play a major role in the on-going creation and procreation of human life in this world.

Mothers were recognized as important persons, who were entitled to great respect for a variety of reasons in several other biblical traditions.[10] Many texts refer to both mothers and fathers in this way. Thus the Fifth Commandment: "Honor your father and your mother, [so] that your days may be long in the land which YHWH your God gives you."[11] Children who violated this commandment to the extent of striking or cursing either parent could be subject to capital punishment.[12] Likewise, children were expected to obey the "voice" of both their mothers and their fathers,

9. See Silvia Schroer, "Feminist Reconstruction," 147–49 (discussing related issues and interpretations).

10. Compare Scholz, *Women's Hebrew Bible*, 66–70 (discussing feminist interpretations that recognize the positive characterization of mothers in various biblical texts). Scholz suggests that feminist interpreters may be ambivalent as to biblical motherhood: whether women found at least partial personal fulfillment as mothers, or whether bearing children was an unwelcome task thrust upon them by the dominant patriarchy.

11. Exod 20:12; See Deut 5:16. And see Deut 27:16: "'Cursed be he who dishonors his father or mother.' And all the people shall say, 'Amen.'" See also Sir 7:27–28.

12. Exod 21:15, 17. See also Lev 20:9 ("[E]veryone who curses his father or his mother shall be put to death"). Several proverbs, however, indicate that although such offenses against parents were still considered serious, in later times the death penalty was no longer applied. See Prov 19:26; 20:20; and 30:11.

and strict procedures were spelled out for dealing with sons who refused
to do so.[13]

Many proverbs hold mothers in high esteem, emphasizing, among
other things, their shared authority and status in the family structure.[14]
Thus, for instance, Proverbs 6:20:

> My son, keep your father's commandment,
>   and forsake not your mother's teaching.[15]

Some sayings address not only sons, but children generally. For example,
Sirach 3:1–4:

> Listen to me your father, O children;
>   and act accordingly, that you may be kept in safety.
> For the Lord honored the father above the children,
>   and he confirmed the right of the mother over her sons.
> Whoever honors his father atones for sins,
>   and whoever glorifies his mother is like one who lays up treasure.

Several other proverbs also refer to fathers and mothers in language indicating that they were equally and importantly involved in their children's
lives; for instance:

> A wise son makes a glad father,
>   but a foolish son is a sorrow to his mother. (Prov 10:1)[16]

> A foolish son is a grief to his father
>   and bitterness to her who bore him. (Prov 17:25)[17]

---

13. See Deut 21:18–21, considered below in chapter 8.

14. See Starr, *Bible Status*, 75–76: "Under Mosaic legislation, father and mother stand
side by side. In Old Testament literature, wherever honor and obedience to parents are
commanded, the names of 'father and mother' are conjoined." See also Bird, "Images of
Women," 57: "In Proverbs, as in the laws, the mother is described in positive terms only.
But here it is clear that the term 'mother' does not refer primarily to her reproductive
function but to her role in the nurture and education of the child. She is not merely the
womb that bears a man but a source of wisdom essential to life."

15. Other sayings that emphasize a mother's authority over her children include Prov
30:17 and Sir 3:5–16.

16. See also Prov 15:20. The NRSV reads "child" instead of "son" in both texts.

17. See also Prov 23:22, 25; 28:24. In these texts also the NRSV uses gender inclusive
language instead of "son" or "he."

And children should remember and be guided by the moral teachings and example of both parents.[18] Wisdom, represented in biblical tradition as a woman,[19] is also compared to a mother: "[H]e who holds to the law will obtain wisdom. She will come to meet him like a mother" (Sir 15:1–2). In addition, it is noteworthy that biblical tradition reflects appreciation and respect for mothers in many kinds of animal and bird species.[20]

DAUGHTERS

Daughters are regarded positively,[21] but also sometimes as cause for parental concern. Laban, compelled by circumstances to part from his daughters who were now Jacob's wives and going away with him, cautions Jacob not to ill-treat them or take any additional wives besides his daughters (Gen 31:43–50). "Daughter" is a term of endearment in the book of Ruth,[22] and also in the New Testament.[23] The prophet Nathan's parable about the rich man and his many herds, and the poor man and his one little pet lamb points to the affection men typically may have felt for their daughters.[24]

18. See, e.g., Prov 1:8–9; 6:20–22; Sir 23:14; 41:17.

19. See, e.g., Prov 3:13–20; 8:22–9:12; Wis 9:9—11:1; Sir 24:1–22.

20. See, e.g., Exod 22:30; 23:19b; 34:26b; Lev 22:28; and Deut 14:21b (domestic animal mothers in relation to their young); 2 Esd 2:15; 4 Macc 14:13–17; and Matt 23:37 = Luke 13:34 (mother birds caring for their young).

21. But see Gen 19:4–8, where Lot offers his two virgin daughters to the depraved men of Sodom who lusted after his male guests. Lot's conduct was not presented as a model for Israelite practice, nor was his subsequent incestuous, albeit unconscious, intercourse with these same daughters, which resulted in the births of the "fathers" of the Moabites and the Ammonites (Gen 19:3–9). See discussion by Frymer-Kensky, *Reading Women*, 258–63. See also Judg 11:29–40, describing the tragic vow of Jephthah, which led him to sacrifice his daughter, his only child. The story's pathos is grounded on Jephthah's affection for this daughter, and hers for him. See Trible, *Texts of Terror*, 92–116, and Frymer-Kensky, *Reading Women*, 107–17.

22. See Ruth 1:11–13; 2:8; 3:10–11. And see Ruth 4:15: "[Y]our daughter-in-law who loves you, . . . is more to you than seven sons . . ."

23. See Matt 9:22; Mark 5:34; Luke 8:48.

24. See 2 Sam 12:1–3. Compare Sirach's dour observation: "It is a disgrace to be the father of an undisciplined son, and the birth of a daughter is a loss" (Sir 22:3). See Starr, *Bible Status*, 77–81, on daughters in biblical tradition, particularly Starr's analysis of Num 30:3–5, 16, as to father's authority to over-rule religious vows by daughters who were minors. And see below, note 41. Interpreters generally do not notice that the daughters referred to in Num 30 are minors, still living in their fathers' homes (Num 30:3). In

Several proverbs show that men were concerned about their daughters' welfare. Seeing them married to the right kind of husband was important:

> Do you have daughters? Be concerned for their chastity,
> and do not show yourself too indulgent with them.
> Give a daughter in marriage; you will have finished a great task.
> But give her to a man of understanding. (Sir 7:24–25)

But girls will be girls:

> A sensible daughter obtains her husband,
> but one who acts shamefully brings grief to her father.
> An impudent daughter disgraces father and husband,
> and will be despised by both. (Sir 22:4–5)

Other texts in Sirach call on fathers to "keep watch" over "headstrong" daughters, both for their own good, and lest they bring notoriety and shame.[25] Evidently daughters were not uniformly deferential to fathers' wishes. Yet while ungovernable sons might be subject to capital punishment (Deut 21:18–21), there is no such law as to disobedient daughters. Laws pertaining to the rights or interests of daughters will be considered below.[26]

WIVES

After eating the forbidden fruit, the primordial man and his wife try to hide from YHWH-God "among the trees of the garden" (Gen 3:8). Asked why they had eaten the fruit, the man blames the woman, and the woman blames the serpent (Gen 3:12–13). The sequel consists of a series of etiological explanations for latter-day phenomena: why snakes have no legs, why men have to labor in order to grow their food, and why humans are mortal. In this context, YHWH-God tells the woman that she shall experience pain in childbirth; moreover: "Your desire shall be for your husband, and he shall rule over you" (Gen 3:16). The text does not command the woman to be subject to her husband's rule; rather, it

---

modern Anglo-American law, minors likewise are considered to lack legal capacity, e.g., to sign binding contracts.

25. Sir 26:10–12 and 42:11. See also Sir 42:9–10, describing other ways daughters worry their fathers and rob them of sleep with worry over them.

26. See below, chapters 6, 10, and 11.

tries to explain why husbands were thought to exercise such authority.[27] However, it might be noted that the text, as written, refers only to this primordial woman and her husband; it says nothing about relations between husbands and wives in later generations. It may be significant that no subsequent Old Testament or New Testament text tries to justify male dominance by reference to Genesis 3:16. And no other Old Testament text even suggests that wives should be subject to their husbands. Nor, as has been mentioned, are there any Old Testament accounts of wives being subject to their husbands.[28]

Modern interpreters sometimes urge (or assert) that in biblical times, men regarded and treated their wives as mere "property." This suggestion usually is based on the observation that in Exodus 20:17, the Tenth Commandment lists "the neighbor's wife" after "the neighbor's house" and before "servants" and other things belonging to the neighbor.[29] The suggestion would be more persuasive if there were any biblical laws, narratives, or sayings in which wives were portrayed as property. There are none.[30] Perhaps in order to correct any such inference that might be

27. As to Gen 3:16, see Sloane, "And he shall rule." As to etiological stories in the Bible, see Hiers, *Trinity Guide*, 37–40; and Gunkel, *Legends of Genesis*.

28. See above, chapters 1 and 2. In fact, wives sometimes appear as the dominant partner. In this connection, see also Amos 4:1, addressing wealthy, perhaps suburbanite, Israelite women: "Hear this word, you cows of Bashan, who are in the mountain of Samaria, who oppress the poor, who crush the needy, who say to their husbands, 'Bring, that we may drink!'"

29. See, e.g., Ebeling, *Women's Lives*, 83. Nevertheless, Ebeling adds: "Women were not simply property that could be bought and sold, however, and nowhere is a man's absolute sovereignty over his wife indicated in the biblical text." Ibid. Concubines probably were regarded as property, and could be subject to abuse by their owners or others. Abuse was condemned, in Judg 19–20, which culminates in all the other "tribes" of Israel committing genocide against the people of Benjamin as punishment for the gruesome abuse of a Levite's concubine. (See Judg 20:1–10) This narrative, and the subsequent expressions of depravity described in Judg 21, were said to illustrate what was happening "[i]n those days [when] there was no king in Israel; [and] every man did what was right in his own eyes." Judg 21:25. See Frymer-Kensky's insightful account of these events, *Reading Women*, 118–38.

30. See generally Wright, *God's People*, 183–221, reviewing recent secondary literature, and examining pertinent biblical texts. Compare Bird, "Images of Women," 42: "In some texts the woman of ancient Israel is portrayed simply as a class of property." See also, Hollyday, *Clothed with the Sun*, 5: "In ancient Israel, women were considered property, first of their fathers, and then of their husbands." Slaves, both male and female, are regarded as property in some texts (such as Lev 25:44–46); however a number of laws also recognized them as persons. See, e.g., Exod 21:7–11, 26–27; and Deut 15:12–18,

drawn from the Exodus sequence, the Deuteronomic version of the Tenth Commandment mentions "the neighbor's wife" first, in what appears to be a special and separate category, and then goes on to list various types of property: "Neither shall you covet your neighbor's wife; and you shall not desire your neighbor's house, his field, . . . or anything that is your neighbor's" (Deut 5:21).[31] Some of the wisdom texts quoted below characterize a good wife as "a good thing," "far more precious than jewels," her husband's "crown," and "his best possession." However, the contexts and related sayings show that these texts mean that such wives were regarded as highly valued persons, not as "property." Likewise, texts that refer to a man's wife[32] merely describe their relationship; they do not mean that a man owned his wife. Similarly, many texts characterize a woman's husband as *her* husband.[33]

Good wives are considered among the greatest blessings of men's lives, and as the source of all kinds of both tangible and intangible benefits. Among many shorter sayings, the following express admiration and appreciation:

Do not deprive yourself of a wise and good wife,
for her charm is worth more than gold. (Sir 7:19)[34]

He who finds a good wife finds a good thing,
and obtains favor from YHWH. (Prov 18:22)

---

considered below in chapters 6 and 7. So also Westbrook, "Female Slave." See generally, Boecker, *Law and Administration*, 155–63, and Wright, *God's People*, 239–59.

31. So also Burrows, *Outline*, 298: "Where the tenth commandment, according to Exodus, forbids coveting a neighbor's house, wife, slaves, or cattle, Deuteronomy sets the wife distinctly apart from the property, as though to avoid any possible misunderstanding." And see below, note 40.

32. See, e.g., Gen 3:17; 12:17–20; 17:15, 19. Interpreters sometimes urge that Abraham and Isaac treated their wives, Sarah and Rebekah, as "property" when they passed them off as "sisters" in order to save their own necks (Gen 12:10–20; 20:1–18; 26:6–11). There is no indication in these texts that anyone considered these women *property*. In these stories the men clearly mistreated their *wives*; however, Sarah and Rebekah obviously endured the indignities for the sake of their husbands. The narrator's intent in telling these stories is not certain; but among other things, the stories underscore these women's attractiveness (to foreign potentates), and divine providence in restoring them to their husbands.

33. E.g., Gen 3:16; 29:34; 30:15; 2 Kgs 4:9, 22; Prov 7:19; Amos 4:1; Jdt 8:2; 16:22–24; Sir 25:18, 22–23.

34. See also Eccl 9:9: "Enjoy life with the wife you love, all the days of your vain life which he has given you under the sun . . ."

> House and wealth are inherited from fathers,
>> but a prudent wife is from YHWH. (Prov 19:14)

> Happy is he who lives with an intelligent wife. (Sir 25:8)

These themes are developed in greater detail in a series of more extended texts. The following excerpts from such texts are fairly typical:

> A good wife who can find?
>> She is far more precious than jewels . . .
> Strength and dignity are her clothing,
>> and she laughs at the time to come.
> She opens her mouth with wisdom,
>> and the teaching of kindness is on her tongue . . .
> Her children rise up and call her blessed;
>> her husband also, and he praises her:
> "Many women have done excellently,
>> but you surpass them all." (Prov 31:10, 25–26, 28–29)[35]

> Happy is the husband of a good wife;
>> the number of his days will be doubled.
> A loyal wife rejoices her husband,
>> and he will complete his years in peace.
> A good wife is a great blessing;
>> she will be granted among the blessings of the man
>> who fears YHWH.
> Whether rich or poor, his heart is glad,
>> and at all times his face is cheerful. (Sir 26:1–4)[36]

A good wife was considered a great blessing; but wives were not always considered good:

> A good wife is the crown of her husband,
>> but she who brings shame is like rottenness in his bones. (Prov 12:4)

35. Excerpts from the longer discourse at Prov 31:10–31. Some feminist interpreters express ambivalence as to this portrayal of the "good wife." Here she is credited with numerous positive qualities and abilities. But is her status only "auxiliary," merely that of a "good investment"? See Carmody, *Biblical Woman*, 72–73. Compare Starr, *Bible Status*, 75: "The thirty-first chapter of Proverbs formed no part of Mosaic legislation, but was an outgrowth of that system which assigned to woman honorable place in the life of the nation. The author of this inspired production was a woman—the mother of King Lemuel." Whether or not there ever was an historical King Lemuel, Prov 31 is explicitly attributed to a woman. See Prov 31:1–2.

36. See also Sir 25:1; 26:13–18; and 36:24, which reads: "He who acquires a wife gets his best possession, a helper fit for him and a pillar of support."

Several other texts warn against the dire effects of being married to the wrong kind of wife. Those quoted or cited here suggest that men were not necessarily "masters" or "lords" in their own homes.

> It is better to live in a corner of the housetop
> than in a house shared with a contentious woman. (Prov 21:9)[37]

The King James Version renders the text less delicately:

> It is better to dwell in the corner of the housetop
> than with a brawling woman in a wide house. (Prov 21:9, KJV)

A few other proverbs are in similar vein:

> A continual dripping on a rainy day
> and a contentious woman are alike;
> to restrain her is to restrain the wind
> or to grasp oil in his right hand. (Prov 27:15–16)[38]

Some sayings in Sirach are even more vivid. For example:

> I would rather dwell with a lion and a dragon
> than dwell with an evil wife.
> The wickedness of a wife changes her appearance,
> and darkens her face like that of a bear.
> Her husband takes his meals among the neighbors,
> and he cannot help sighing bitterly. (Sir 25:16–18)[39]

Nevertheless, husbands should respect and be gentle with their wives:

> Do not be jealous of the wife of your bosom,
> and do not teach her an evil lesson to your own hurt. (Sir 9:1)

And husbands were expected to support their wives, rather than the other way around:

> There is wrath and impudence and great disgrace
> when a wife supports her husband. (Sir 25:22)

---

37. See also Prov 21:19; 25:24. Compare the folk proverb in the American South: "Mama ain't happy, ain't nobody happy." Similar version quoted in Mickle, *Replacing Dad*, ix (unnumbered page).

38. See also Prov 19:13b.

39. See also Sir 25:19–20, 23; 26:6–9.

On the basis of the texts considered here, it can be said with some certainty that under biblical law, and the cultural norms undergirding it, wives were not regarded as property;[40] nor were biblical wives expected to be subservient or subordinate to their husbands.[41]

WIDOWS

Interpreters sometimes conjecture that in biblical times, widows often may have been sold into slavery by their relatives.[42] There is no textual support for this conjecture in the Old Testament. But it is likely that widows often lacked adequate means of support, and were subject to abuse by predatory elements in the community. Many laws and other biblical texts indicate concern for widows' welfare.[43]

---

40. See Burrows, *Outline*, 294: "The form of the marriage arrangement is . . . that of a covenant between the families of the bridegroom and the bride, brought about and sealed by the presentation of gifts, especially a gift from the bridegroom or his father to the father of the bride. The obvious resemblance between this practice and the acquisition of property by paying a price for it accounts for the common but inaccurate idea that Hebrew marriage was marriage by purchase."

41. So also Starr, *Bible Status*, 99: "In closing this study of the domestic status of women under the Mosaic regime, we throw out challenge to any reader to produce any edict from the Levitical code, aside from Numbers xxx: 30:6–8, 12–15, that even implied the subordination of the wife, and in this particular case the supervision allowed was restricted, and served for relief even more than for restraint." See above, note 24. According to Num 30:6–15, a husband could void a wife's "vow or any thoughtless utterance . . . by which she has bound herself," or "any binding oath to afflict herself." The text apparently refers only to religious vows. Compare Fiorenza, "Patriarchal Traditions," 41: "In the Hebrew patriarchal society, women were totally dependent on their fathers and husbands. Numbers 30:2–12, for example, demonstrates the complete dependency and subordination of a daughter or a wife, not only in familial-cultural affairs but also in religious matters." Undoubtedly single women in biblical times were at greater risk than women who had fathers, husbands, or other relatives to care for them and protect their interests. The same seems true in any society, ancient or modern.

42. Schroer, "Feminist Reconstruction," 123. See also Hollyday, *Clothed with the Sun*, 13: "Widows were often blamed for their own state, considered a disgrace, harshly treated, and sometimes enslaved." Neither Schroer nor Hollyday cites any textual support for these contentions.

43. Such laws, Frymer-Kensky suggests, were "predicated on the assumption of patriarchy: the widow is dependent on the concern and good will of males only because she herself has no real property." "Bible and Women's Studies," 17. As will be noted below in chapters 9, 10, and 11, many biblical texts refer to widows (and other women) who apparently owned real property (including houses and/or land).

Such concern comes to expression in both exhortations and laws. As to the former, for example:

> Be like a father to orphans,
>> and instead of a husband to their mother;
> you will then be like a son of the Most High,
>> and he will love you more than does your mother. (Sir 4:10)[44]

A number of laws aimed at protecting widows from oppression or exploitation. Widows were one of the classes of persons whose rights and interests were affirmed by biblical social welfare legislation.[45] Under terms of Deuteronomy 24:19–22, land owners were obliged to leave portions of their harvests from fields, olive orchards, and vineyards for "the sojourner, the fatherless, and the widow."[46] Gleaning by widows is illustrated in the book of Ruth (Ruth 2). Several other kinds of laws likewise were meant to provide food for widows. Food was to be shared with widows and others in need at the "feast of weeks" and the "feast of booths" or "ingathering" at which times, "every man shall give as he is able" (Deut 16:9–17).[47] In addition, biblical law called for a triennial tithe on all produce. These tithes were to be "laid up" in each town, creating local food banks: "At the end of every three years you shall bring forth all the tithe of your produce in the same year, and lay it up within your towns; and the Levite, because he has no portion or inheritance with you, and the sojourner, the fatherless, and the widow, who are within your towns, shall come and eat and be filled; that YHWH your God may bless you in all the work of your hands that you do." (Deut 14:28–29).[48] This arrangement would have provided a supply of food all year, and each of the two following years, until produce

44. See also Isa 1:16–17; and Job 29:13, where, among his other good deeds, Job recalls: "I caused the widow's heart to sing for joy." See also Job 31:16. Compare Schroer, "Feminist Reconstruction," 141: "On every page of the book of Job, one may study the deficits of the male-dominated religion of YHWH after the Exile."

45. On the broader subject of biblical social legislation, see Hiers, *Justice and Compassion*, 165–218.

46. See also Lev 19:9–10 and 23:22, so providing for "the poor" generally.

47. This last requirement could be construed as precedent for such latter-day arrangements as graduated income taxes.

48. See also Deut 26:12–15. These laws could be seen as precedent for such modern social welfare programs as Aid to Families with Dependent Children (AFDC), Women, Infants and Children (WIC), food stamps, and other government sponsored assistance to persons in need, as well as for private, charitable relief agencies.

was gathered and stored at the next triennial tithe.[49] It may be significant that the tithe was intended to provide direct assistance in the form of food for those who, for whatever reason, were in need; it was not meant to provide support for religious institutions. Also, it may be noticed that the language of this and other welfare laws just mentioned was mandatory, not merely precatory or hortatory.

Another type of law concerned provisions for women whose husbands died without leaving a son to look after their surviving widows. This is the law of "levirate marriage," set out in Deuteronomy 25:5–10.[50] In brief, this law provides that when brothers live together and one of them dies without leaving a son, the surviving brother is obliged to marry the widow and have a son on behalf of the deceased.[51] In the story of Judah and Tamar (Gen 38), the obligation apparently was extended to the widow's father-in-law, and in the story of Ruth, to the nearest male relative.[52] Thus the widow would be assured of support by her new husband during his lifetime,[53] and if a son is born to this couple, by that son if or when the new husband predeceased her.[54]

The texts considered in Part I of this book show that in biblical times women were portrayed as powerful and important people, even if not always in positive terms. Part II takes up the question whether, given this cultural and normative context, women were understood to have any of the same kinds of legal rights as male members of the community, and particularly, whether they enjoyed what in modern Western jurisprudence is referred to as legal capacity.

---

49. Evidently many kinds of food could be stored for such periods of time. See Lev 25:20–23 (three years) and Gen 41 (seven years).

50. See Brin, *Studies in Biblical Law*, 58–60; and Hiers, *Justice and Compassion*, 40–43, 199–202, also citing other pertinent secondary literature. And see below, chapters 6 and 8.

51. In modern parlance, the *levir* (Latin, for brother-in-law) could be characterized as such a son's surrogate father.

52. Related aspects of these stories are considered below in chapters 8 and 11. It cannot be determined whether the stories of Judah and Tamar and of Ruth and "the *go'el*" (or "redeemer") represent extensions of the obligation to such other relatives, or whether the law at Deut 25:5–10 was intended to limit the persons obligated under earlier common law or practice to the deceased's brother-in-law.

53. See Ruth 3:1–5.

54. See Ruth 4:13–17. Here it is anticipated that the new son would care for his *grand-mother* in *her* old age.

PART TWO

The Rights and Legal Status
of Women in Biblical Law

FROM THE FOREGOING, IT appears that in biblical times women generally were regarded as persons who were due respect and consideration on the part of others in the larger community. In that case, it would not be surprising to find that biblical law treated women as persons entitled to at least some rights and legal status. The next several chapters examine biblical texts relating to certain categories of such rights and status.

Chapter 6 identifies a number of rights described in biblical traditions as inhering in, or perhaps more aptly, providing for the interests and welfare of women. Chapter 7 considers laws that now might be characterized as calling for "equal protection," that is, laws that benefited males and females equally. Many of these laws explicitly applied to women. Then in chapters 8 through 11, attention turns to what, in modern Anglo-American jurisprudence, would be called the question of women's legal capacity, that is, the status deemed necessary for a person to take actions that courts recognize as legally effective. In these chapters, it is observed that men and women enjoyed equal legal capacity with respect to several types of actions.

Chapter 8 reviews biblical laws that expressly allowed, or even required women to appear and testify in court under various circumstances, and points to several biblical narratives where women reportedly did so. Chapter 9 focuses on texts indicating that women could be parties to legally binding contracts, and, related to this, that women had the legal capacity to purchase, own, and sell property. Chapter 10 describes texts where women were the beneficiaries of wills or bequests, and one text where a woman bequeathed property to other persons.

Chapter 11 takes up the topic of inheritance "by operation of law" or the "laws of intestate succession," in particular, the biblical law providing for inheritance by daughters. This chapter also takes note of substantial evidence that, in biblical times, widows inherited property from their husbands. Chapter 12 summarizes the book's main findings as to the rights and status of women under biblical law. The final chapter points to certain ways that Old Testament tradition and law provide important perspectives that challenge contemporary cultural values, social policies, and legal practices.

6

Women's Rights

> Women without children were protected by levirate marriage . . .
> This was seen as a widow's right, and perhaps the only chance a
> woman would have for security after the death of her husband.
>
> —Jennie R. Ebeling

BIBLICAL TRADITIONS MENTION ONLY a few rights specifically.[1] Other rights are implicit in laws and admonitions that impose or invoke duties or obligations on the community and particular members of it. As corollary to these obligations, several classes of persons are, in effect, endowed with certain rights. Other rights will be considered in the following chapters.

The laws examined in this chapter all have to do with women's rights in situations where they could have been at risk in one way or another. Some of these laws expressly referred to widows and, in various ways, were intended to protect their interests. For example, Exodus 22:22–23: "You shall not afflict any widow or orphan. If you do afflict them, and they cry to me, I will surely hear their cry; and my wrath will burn . . ." The implication is that widows, along with orphans, had the right to be

---

1. See generally Wolfson, "Rights Theory and Jewish Law"; and Patrick, *Old Testament Law*, 65–72, 85–87, 92, 128–29, 134–36, 163–64. "Rights" are mentioned in Prov 29:7: "A righteous man knows the rights of the poor; a wicked man does not understand such knowledge," and in Prov 31:9: "Open your mouth, judge righteously, maintain the rights of the poor and needy." The underlying Hebrew term is *dîn*, which means "cause for judgment." Davidson, *Hebrew and Chaldee Lexicon*, CXLVII–CXLVIII. Compare the modern legal equivalent expression: "cause of action." In these contexts, "rights" appears to be a fair translation. Widows often were among the "poor" and "needy."

free from affliction or oppression.[2] Widows' clothing was not to be taken as collateral to secure loans: "You shall not pervert the justice due to the sojourner or to the fatherless, or take a widow's garment in pledge" (Deut 4:17).[3] Here it is implied that widows had the right not to be required to give over their clothes as collateral.

Various biblical social welfare laws obliged landowners to allow widows to glean agricultural products from the owners' fields, orchards, and vineyards, while other laws provided for widows to share in the distribution of food at periodic harvest festivals and from food banks supplied by the third-year tithe. Such laws implied that widows, along with the others thereby provided for, had the right to enjoy these benefits.[4] In modern discourse, these benefits might be classified as "entitlements" or as a "safety net" for persons in need of assistance.

Four other laws provided protections for women in particular circumstances where they might otherwise have been vulnerable to injury or abuse. Each required other persons in the community to treat these women with consideration. In each case, the laws either imply or specify that women in such circumstances were entitled to certain rights. One of these laws, known as the law of levirate marriage (Deut 25:5–10), already has been considered.[5] This law provided a form of "social security" for widows, by establishing that those whose husbands had died without leaving sons and who might not otherwise be able to support themselves, had the right to marry and be cared for by the deceased's brother (or other male relative).[6] His refusal to marry the widow was a violation of "the

2. See Isa 1:16–17: "Cease to do evil, learn to do good; seek justice, correct oppression; defend the fatherless, plead for the widow." See also Deut 10:18; 27:19; Isa 1:23; Jer 5:28; 7:5–6; Zech 7:9–10; Mal 3:5; Ps 94:1–7; Prov15:25; and Sir 4:9–10; 35:14.

3. See also Deut 27:19: "Cursed be anyone who deprives the alien, the orphan, and the widow of justice." And see Exod 22:25–27; Deut 24:12–15, as to rights of the poor generally.

4. See above, chapter 5 (widows), and below, chapter 8. And see Isa 10:1–2 quoted below in chapter 11 (referring to the "right[s] of the poor"), and Jer 5:28 (the rights of the needy"). See also, Hiers, "Biblical Social Welfare Legislation," 66–74.

5. See above, chapter 5 (widows). See also Ebeling, *Women's Lives*, 134: "Women without children were protected by levirate marriage . . . This was seen as a widow's right, and perhaps the only chance a woman would have for security after the death of her husband." See also Otto, "False Weights," 138–40.

6. Compare Schroer, "Feminist Reconstruction," 123: "Israelite men clearly reneged on their duty on many occasions." Schroer does not explain how it can be determined that such was clearly the case.

duty of a husband's brother" owed *to her* (Deut 25:7). As is indicated by Deuteronomy 25:6, which implies that more children might be born later, the law evidently presumes that the levirate marriage would continue after the birth of the first son.

What might be described as a tort law, set out in Exodus 21:22–25, stated that if a pregnant woman was injured by brawling men, the man who did the harm should be subjected to punishment equivalent to the nature of the injury. Here we see one of the biblical laws that commentators commonly refer to as the *"lex talionis."*[7] This law implies that pregnant women had a right to freedom from bodily harm. Clearly the safety and well being of pregnant women was a matter of concern under this law. As will be seen in the following chapter, different versions of the *lex talionis* protected women in two other kinds of situations.

Another law detailed procedures that were to be followed if a man sold his daughter as a maid servant or slave (Heb.: 'amah'). This law, found in Exodus 21:7–11, provides a series of protections for such daughters.[8] Like many other laws, this one evidently was intended to reform existing customary practices.[9] The context suggests that normally the young woman would have become the purchaser's wife, or at least his concubine. If the purchaser became displeased with her, he must allow her to be "redeemed." Alternatively, he might give her to his son as a wife or concubine, but in that he case must treat her as his daughter. If he keeps her as his own wife, and marries another woman, the purchaser must not "diminish her food, her clothing, or her marital rights"[10] (Exod 21:10). If

7. See Hiers, *Justice and Compassion*, 90–91; and generally, 154–55, as to the biblical *lex talionis*. See also Westbrook and Wells, *Everyday*, 76–77, noting problems of translation and interpretation, and discussing somewhat similar provisions in other ancient Near Eastern law codes.

8. There is no indication as to the circumstances under which a man might have sold his daughter. Most likely it would have been because he was in debt. See Westbrook and Wells, *Everyday Law*, 64–65, 114, and 132. This law could be read to mean that men regarded their daughters as "property." If so, daughters were not the only persons to be so regarded. According to Neh 5:3–5, economic hardship had caused some people to sell both sons and daughters as debt slaves. Moreover, men might even sell themselves as debt slaves. See Lev 25:39–55, setting out certain conditions, and arrangements for redemption.

9. See generally, Hiers, *Justice and Compassion*, 209–11, and Westbrook, "Female Slave," 218–20, 235–36.

10. Heb.: 'onah, a *hapax* word, perhaps meaning "conjugal rights" or "cohabitation." Davidson, *Hebrew and Chaldee Lexicon*, DXCI. Since "marital rights" are mentioned in

he does not provide these three things for her, "she shall go out for nothing, without payment of money" (Exod 21:11). It would be strange if a young women who had been sold as a slave or maid servant was entitled to such rights, while free women in the same society were not so entitled.[11] Therefore, it is reasonable to infer that all wives, not just those who had been purchased as servants or slaves, were entitled to such rights under customary or common law: at a minimum: food, clothes, and her marital rights—or oil.

Deuteronomy 21:10–14 concerns women taken as captives during times of war. Taking such women as wives, among other spoils of battle, probably had been common practice since early times. The law evidently was intended to mitigate the consequences of this practice.[12] It provides that when an Israelite man sees among the captives a woman whom he wishes to take for his wife, he may do so, but he must treat her with consideration, including allowing her time for grieving before consummating the marriage. If he decides that he does not wish to keep her, he still must treat her with respect: "Then, if you have no delight in her, you shall let her go where she will; but you shall not sell her for money, you shall not treat her as a slave, since you have humiliated her" (Deut 21:14). In effect, this law establishes the captive woman's right to some measure of freedom, if not total emancipation.[13] As will be seen in the following chapter, biblical law also provided certain rights for slave women as well as for slave men.

Biblical law recognized that women had many other rights as well. These will be described below in chapter 7, as instances of "equal protec-

---

addition to food and clothing, it could be inferred that "marital rights" refers to other benefits, including what, in modern—somewhat delicate, if slightly archaic—legal terminology is referred to as the "right of consortium." Compare Patrick, *Old Testament Law*, 71: the right to "the possibility of bearing children." But see Westbrook, "Female Slave," 218, translating *'onah* as "oil." As to biblical laws and customs relating to marriage, dowry, and divorce, see, e.g., Burrows' classic study, *The Basis of Israelite Marriage*; Ebeling, *Women's Lives*, 79–94; Hiebert, "Whence Shall Help Come"; Pressler, *View of Women*, and "Wives and Daughters"; and Williams, "Insult to Injury?"

11. See Westbrook, "Female Slave," 236: "The duty of a husband to provide his wife with sustenance was so self-evident that it went virtually unmentioned in ancient Near Eastern sources."

12. See Otto, "False Weights," 140–45.

13. See Westbrook and Wells, *Everyday Law*, 64: "[H]aving married her, [he] may not re-enslave her, should he subsequently divorce her." See also Westbrook, "Female Slave," 235.

tion"; and in chapters 8 through 11, which examine various aspects of women's "legal capacity" in biblical times. The biblical text, of course, does not use the terms "equal protection" and "legal capacity." These terms, however, aptly characterize many laws and legal practices described in biblical tradition. We turn now to laws providing "equal protection" for women—that is, laws that gave women the same rights or status as those enjoyed by men.

7

Equal Protection

[T]he Bible did not justify social inequality by an ideology of superiority or otherness. On the contrary, the Bible's explicit ideology
presents a unified vision of humankind wherein women and men
were created in the image of God.

—Tikva Frymer-Kensky

A NUMBER OF LAWS make it clear that in a wide range of circumstances,
women were entitled to the same rights or protections as men.[1] In
modern legal parlance, these laws might be classified under the heading
of "equal protection," or, in some instances, as laws prohibiting invidious
gender-based discrimination.

Some of these laws concern the rights or interests of parents—both
parents. The Decalogue's Fifth Commandment calls for honoring both
"your father and your mother" (Exod 20:12; Deut 5:16). Thus also,
Deuteronomy 27:16: "Cursed be anyone who dishonors father or mother"
(NRSV). Sons, and possibly daughters, who cursed or struck either of

---

1. See generally, Cohn, *Human Rights in Jewish Law*; and Cohn, *Human Rights in
Bible and Talmud*, 80–89. As to women in post-biblical Jewish law, see, e.g., Berkovits,
Jewish Women; Biale, *Women and Jewish Law*; Davidman and Tenenbaum, eds., *Feminist
Perspectives*; and Plaskow, *Standing Again at Sinai*. Lower fees or "valuations" scheduled
in Lev 27:1–8, evidently were meant to make it easier to release females in each age
group from religious vows. See also Num 30:1–16 (circumstances under which fathers
could release their minor daughters from binding vows or pledges, as could husbands
their wives). Reference here is to religious vows or pledges. See also Num 6:2–21; Deut
23:21–23. Compare *NOAB-RSV* annotation: "These cases reflect a society in which woman was subordinate to the man of the family." *NOAB-RSV*, OT section, 204. But see the
more nuanced annotation in the *NOAB-NRSV*, "Hebrew Bible" section, 230, captioned
"Women's vows." See also above, chapter 5 nn. 24 and 41.

their parents, could be subject to capital punishment.[2] A son's failure to obey "the voice" of either parent was likewise punishable (Deut 21:18–21).

The Covenant Code (Exod 20–23) contains a series of laws that in modern jurisprudence would be designated "tort" laws.[3] Many of these laws are phrased in gender-neutral language, referring to tort victims as "neighbor" or "owner" (Exod 22:7–15). The NRSV translates references to persons in most of these laws using inclusive terms, such as "whoever" or "someone" (Exod 21:12–17). A few of these laws explicitly apply equally, whether the victims were men or women, adults or children (Exod 21:28–31). The same amount of compensation was to be paid to owners when either a male or a female slave was the victim (Exod 21:32).

Several other laws explicitly provided equal protection for slaves. Male and female slaves alike were to be set free if injured permanently by their owners,[4] and such owners were to be punished equally for fatally striking either a male or female slave.[5] In contrast to the earlier law set out in Exodus 21:1–6, providing for emancipation of male Hebrew slaves (or indentured servants) after six years of service, Deuteronomy 15:12–18 specifically applies to female Hebrew slaves as well. Both male and females slaves thus had the right to be freed after serving for six years. The Deuteronomic law probably was intended to amend the earlier Exodus enactment.[6]

Both men and women could become Nazirites, that is, persons specially consecrated to YHWH (Num 6:2). Those who took "the vow of a Nazirite" came under certain restrictions and were required to present various sacrifices.[7] Nazirites were not priests, but were considered "holy" or separate people. Male and female Nazirites evidently had equal status.

2. Exod 21:15, 17; Lev 20:9.

3. As to biblical tort laws, see Hiers, *Justice and Compassion*, 14–24, and, same author, "Ancient Laws," 480–96.

4. Exod 21:26–27: Specifically, if the owner strikes and destroys a slave's eye, or knocks out his or her tooth. See also Lev 25:6, as to the sabbatical year's providing food for both male and female slaves.

5. Exod 21:20–21. See Westbrook, "Female Slave," 114: "In the legal systems of the ancient Near East, male and female slaves were for the most part subject to the same rules."

6. See Hiers, *Justice and Compassion*, 205–9. See also the biblical fugitive slave law (Deut 23:15–16), which may have been intended to allow not only escaped male, but also escaped female slaves to retain their freedom—and to enjoy open housing—"wherever they please[d]" to reside.

7. Num 6:3–21.

Both the Decalogue and many other biblical laws seem to have been addressed to the entire community of Israel, both male and female members.[8] The Tenth Commandment, which called on men to refrain from coveting their neighbors' wives, is an obvious exception.[9]

Another version of the *lex talionis* provided that if a witness was found to have intentionally and maliciously offered false and adverse testimony in a criminal case, that witness was to be subjected to the same penalty that would have been inflicted upon the person falsely accused.[10] Although the language refers only to false testimony against "a man" or "a brother,"[11] in the late biblical story of Susanna and the Elders, this law was applied against the two men who had falsely and maliciously accused a woman, namely, Susanna.[12] Consequently, "they did to them as they had wickedly planned to do to their neighbor; acting in accordance with the law of Moses, they put them to death."[13]

Likewise, it seems to have been understood that the penalties for mayhem[14] were to be applied against any and all perpetrators, whether the mayhem victims were male or female: "When a man causes a disfigurement in his neighbor, as he has done it shall be done to him, fracture for fracture, eye for eye, tooth for tooth; as he has disfigured a man, he shall be disfigured" (Lev 24:19–20). Since the earlier version of the *lex talionis* considered above[15] was intended specifically to protect pregnant women (and punish men who even unintentionally injured them), it is likely that the mayhem version of this law was meant to protect both male

8. E.g., Exod 19:3–6; 20:21–22; 24:3; Deut 4:44—5:3; 27:1, 9–10; 31:9–14.

9. Exod 20:17; Deut 5:21.

10. Deut 19:16–21.

11. Deut 19:16, 18–19. Compare translation in the NRSV, which generally uses gender inclusive language where arguably so intended: "another," "the other."

12. See Sus vv. 61–62.

13. Sus v. 62. Several biblical laws hold men and women equally responsible and liable for committing the same offenses or types of offense. See, e.g., Lev 20:15–16 (sexual intercourse with an animal); Lev 20:27 (mediums, sorcerers, or wizards); Num 5:6 (wronging another person); Deut 17:2–5 (worship of other gods); Deut 22:5 (wearing the other gender's clothing); Deut 22:22–24 and Lev 20:10 (adultery); and Deut 23:17–18 (neither men nor women to be cult prostitutes).

14. In modern American law, mayhem means causing another person loss of, or the loss of use of any bodily members, or permanent disfigurement. See LaFave, *Criminal Law*, 749–50.

15. Exod 21:22–25. See above, chapter 6.

and female victims injured seriously in other settings. The NRSV's gender inclusive translation, therefore, appears to be justified: "Anyone who maims another shall suffer the same injury in return; fracture for fracture, eye for eye, tooth for tooth; the injury inflicted is the injury to be suffered" (Lev 24:19-20, NRSV).

Moreover, it appears that capital punishment for murder was to be applied whether the murder victim was male or female; at any rate, the NRSV so translates a number of texts, where the Hebrew reference to "a man" may well have been meant to include women victims.[16] Similarly, the prohibition against homicide in the Decalogue is gender-neutral or gender-inclusive: "You shall not kill."[17] Thus, murdering a woman was just as serious a crime as murdering a man, and the punishment would be the same in either case.

In these several respects, biblical law accorded women the same legal status or rights as those enjoyed by men. Yet there were notable exceptions. One was that, at least in early times, men could have more than one wife, while there are no reported instances of polyandry.[18] Also, some of these men, and perhaps others in later times, had female concubines, while there are no indications that women ever had equivalent consorts. Another, somewhat related exception is the fact that while a married woman who engaged in sexual intercourse with a man other than her husband was deemed guilty of adultery, a married man who had sexual relations with a woman other than his wife was not considered guilty of that offense—unless this other woman also was married.[19] Another major

---

16. See, e.g., Gen 9:6; Lev 24:17, 21b, where the NRSV translation refers to killing "a human" or "a human being" rather than killing "a man."

17. Exod 20:13; Deut 5:17.

18. Actually, only a few men were said to have had more than one wife: Lamech (Gen 4:19-23); Abraham, Esau, Jacob, some of the judges in the book of Judges, David, and, most famously, of course, Solomon. Also, perhaps, Ahab, who, it is said, had seventy sons, though most probably were borne by his concubines (2 Kgs 10:1). All of these were in relatively early times, the most recent being kings who lived back in the tenth or ninth centuries BCE. Exodus 21:7-11, referring to a possible second wife, also dates from this early period. See Biale, *Women and Jewish Law*, 50: "[I]n the Bible the practice of polygany seems to be limited to the Patriarchs and the kings, and as a rule we do not hear of it in the life of the common man." Concubines are mentioned only in early traditions.

A man who, under the law of levirate marriage (Deut 25:5-10) acted in the role of *levir*, by providing his brother's or near relative's widow with a son, *might* already have a wife, but none of the biblical accounts of levirate marriage mentions such a wife.

19. See Hiers, *Justice and Compassion*, 97-99. On the other hand, although male homosexual relations were considered "an abomination" and subject to capital punish-

gender-based inequality is that under the law set out at Deuteronomy 24:1, a man could divorce his wife "if she finds no favor in his eyes because he has found some indecency in her." Interpreters offer several suggestions as to the meaning of this language,[20] but there is no counterpart law providing for a woman to divorce her husband.

Two other laws notably failed to protect women's interests, though applying to both the men and the women involved. Exodus 22:16 reads: "If a man seduces a virgin who is not betrothed, and lies with her, he shall give the marriage present for her, and make her his wife." The woman's father could refuse to allow the marriage (Exod 22:17), but there is no provision for the woman herself to refuse.[21] The other law, in Deuteronomy 22:28–29, says in effect, that if a man seizes and rapes "a virgin who is not betrothed," he must marry her "because he has violated her";[22] moreover, he may not afterwards divorce her. Here, again, there is no provision for the woman to refuse to marry the man—a more serious omission here, since in such cases the woman had not consented to the sexual encounter in the first place. These laws may have been intended to keep young women from being victimized sexually, and to assure that men who either seduced or sexually assaulted them would have to care for them as husbands, rather than abandoning them with damaged reputations, along with any children so conceived.[23] But neither law respected the women's own wishes.[24] Nor, for that matter, those of the man.[25]

---

ment (Lev 20:13), there is no biblical law prohibiting or condemning lesbian or female homosexual relations.

20. See, e.g., Carmody, *Biblical Woman*, 22–26; and Starr, *Bible Status*, 96–98.

21. Conceivably, the young woman's mother, or possibly the young woman herself, could, if they so wished, tell the father if they considered the "man" unsuitable as a prospective husband. Compare Gen 27:46, where Rebekah tells her husband that she does not want their son to marry certain women, and he does as she asks.

22. Compare Amnon's refusal to marry his half-sister, Tamar, whom he had raped; and David's ineffectual response to the situation. 2 Sam 13:1–22.

23. Burrows, *Outline*, 296, adds a further consideration: "Virginity was demanded of the bride; rape or seduction of an unmarried girl was punished, a betrothed girl being regarded as married. Questions of property rights were clearly involved in these laws, e.g., the father's right to a normal marriage gift for his daughter, which he could not expect if she was not a virgin. For the man there was no such strict requirement of chastity." In those times, there were neither abortion clinics nor homes or shelters for unwed mothers.

24. See Williams, "Insult to Injury?," discussing these and other biblical laws relating to sexual offenses.

25. See ibid, 104–5: "Deuteronomy's treatment of a rape victim is one we would consider inappropriate to her well-being now. However, the message to the man who rapes

Another notable inequality was the fact that ordinarily sons would inherit from their fathers' (or parents') estates, but daughters would not do so unless they had no brothers.[26] Perhaps the most egregious lack of symmetry is found in the notorious law referred to as "the cereal offering of jealousy" (Num 5:11–31), which called for a kind of trial by ordeal if a husband even suspected his wife of infidelity. Again, there is no counterpart provision governing situations where a wife suspects her husband of "going astray and defiling" himself.

Notwithstanding these significant types of unequal protection, in other respects women evidently had many of the same rights as did men. There is no suggestion in biblical tradition that women were inherently inferior to men and on that account not entitled to legal equality.[27] It remains to be considered whether women were also understood to be persons with the same kinds of legal capacity as those enjoyed by men.

In modern Anglo-American law, when a person is said to have legal capacity, the meaning is that such a person has met or attained whatever qualifications are necessary to exercise the same kinds of legal powers as others do in that society.[28] The types of capacity indicated in biblical laws and tradition include the following: the right to appear and testify in court; the capacity to enter into contracts, and to buy, own, or sell property; to receive property as beneficiary of bequests, and, in turn, to bequeath property to others; and, in certain situations, to inherit property under the law or laws of intestate succession. The following chapter takes up the first of these: women's capacity to appear and testify in court.

. . . an unmarried woman is clear: what he has done is a very serious wrong . . . But this at least this can be said: he has been told that what he has done is catastrophically wrong and has consequences that will reverberate for the rest of his life. He cannot gratify his own desires with a woman who cannot (betrothed) or does not (single) consent and expect to walk away scot free." Compare the modern, popular, male rationale, "Butterflies are free."

26. See below, chapter 11. Biblical law did not always disadvantage daughters, however. As has been mentioned, while sons who disobeyed their parents might be subject to capital punishment (Deut 21:18–21), no biblical law calls for the punishment of disobedient daughters.

27. See Frymer-Kensky, "Bible and Women's Studies," 23–24: [T]he Bible did not justify social inequality by an ideology of superiority or otherness. On the contrary, the Bible's explicit ideology presents a unified vision of humankind wherein women and men were created in the image of God." See also same author, *Reading Women*, 337–38.

28. See definition in *Black's Law Dictionary*, quoted above in the Introduction to this book, note 4.

8

Capacity to Appear and Testify in Court

> As with the other family laws the woman was installed by this provision as a legal subject in her own right. Accordingly she was the plaintiff in the local court . . . In this case the widow defended her own right and not that of her deceased husband.
>
> —Eckart Otto

INTERPRETERS SOMETIMES ASSUME THAT under biblical law, women were barred from appearing and testifying in court.[1] The story of Susanna might be read to support this assumption, for there, though accused of adultery, Susanna appears, but does not speak in her own defense.[2] On the other hand, in several other biblical accounts, women do appear in court (or equivalent venues) both on their own behalf, and as witnesses.

---

1. Thus even Boecker, *Law and Administration*, 32: "Women . . . were also excluded from any active part in legal trials." Although Deborah had been an important judge during the period of the judges in early Israel, there do not seem to have been any women among the "elders at the gate." However, women may have served as witnesses to proceedings "at the gate" and possibly as jurors. See Ruth 4:9–11, and Sus vv. 34, 41, 47, 50, 60 ("all the people").

2. It is not said whether Susanna declined to testify in her own behalf, or whether she was prevented from doing so. There is no law or other tradition to the effect that women were not permitted to appear or testify in court, and as will be seen, a number of biblical laws and stories show that women could and often did both. In the OT Apocrypha, the story of Susanna functions to introduce Daniel, who here speaks *pro bono* as Susanna's defense counsel. Had she, herself, spoken, Daniel's appearance would have been, at best, anti-climactic. In short, it appears that from the story teller's standpoint, it was necessary for Susanna to remain silent until after the verdict, in order to set the stage for Daniel's dramatic entrance into the scene.

The earliest account comes at the end of the story of Judah and Tamar in Genesis 38. Judah's oldest son, Er, had married Tamar, but then Er died without having children. Under customary law, the next son, Onan was supposed to marry—at any rate, to impregnate—the widow in order to have "offspring" for his brother.[3] Onan refused to perform the requisite act; and the next younger brother, Shelah, was not yet old enough to do so. Later, after Shelah grew up but still had not married her, Tamar decided to take charge of the situation. She disguised herself as a prostitute and succeeded in attracting her father-in-law Judah's attention. As fee for services rendered, Tamar prudently obtained certain of Judah's distinctive personal items, namely his signet, cord, and staff. In time, after Judah learned of Tamar's pregnancy, he ordered her to be executed for having committed harlotry, or, more likely, adultery.[4] Although there was no formal court proceeding, Tamar now presented her testimony along with the physical evidence (or "exhibits") that resulted in her acquittal: "As she was being brought out, she sent word to her father-in-law, 'By the man to whom these belong, I am with child.' And she said, 'Mark, I pray you, whose these are, the signet and the cord and the staff.' Then Judah acknowledged them and said, 'She is more righteous than I, inasmuch as I did not give her to my son Shelah'" (Gen 38:25–26). Here there was no question whether she had the right to speak and be heard.

The law of levirate marriage itself specifically allows, even requires, a widow in certain circumstances to appear in court (before "the elders at the gate"),[5] and not only to appear, but also to testify, and even take direct action in order to enforce her rights[6]:

---

3. The story either reflects customary or common law, which later was codified in the law of levirate marriage (Deut 25:5–10), or represents a later modification of that law. See Westbrook and Wells, *Everyday Law*, 96: "[T]he intricacies of the levirate law remain a matter of dispute." And see above, chapter 5, note 52, and accompanying text.

4. Even though her first husband was dead, and Onan had evidently declined to marry Tamar, she was nevertheless understood to have been Judah's daughter-in-law, and he, her father-in-law. Gen 38:24–25. Here Judah seems to have been acting as both prosecutor and judge, apparently enforcing customary law against adultery.

5. Although in later times another woman was said to have been an elder (4 Macc 16:14), it is likely that during most of the biblical period only men were elders or judges. As to "the gate" and other courts in biblical tradition, see Boecker, *Laws and Administration*, 31–33.

6. See Otto, "False Weights," 140: "As with the other family laws the woman was installed by this provision as a legal subject in her own right. Accordingly she was the plain-

> If brothers dwell together, and one of them dies and has no son, the wife of the dead shall not be married outside the family to a stranger; her husband's brother shall go in to her, and take her as his wife, and perform the duty of a husband's brother to her. And the first son whom she bears shall succeed to the name of his brother who is dead, that his name may not be blotted out in Israel. And if the man does not wish to take his brother's wife, then his brother's wife shall go up to the gate to the elders, and say, "My husband's brother refuses to perpetuate his brother's name in Israel; he will not perform the duty of a husband's brother to me." Then the elders of his city shall call him, and speak to him: and if he persists, saying, "I do not wish to take her," then his brother's wife shall go up to him in the presence of the elders, and pull his sandal off his foot, and spit in his face; and she shall answer and say, "So shall it be done to the man who does not build up his brother's house." And the name of his house shall be called in Israel, The house of him that had his sandal pulled off. (Deut 25:5–10)

This procedure obviously was intended to put pressure on any reluctant brother-in-law, even to the extent of calling for his being humiliated in public by the widow. The law or practice of levirate marriage served not only to perpetuate the name of the deceased, but, as mentioned previously, to provide for the needs of the widow, who otherwise might have to join the ranks of the indigent.[7] Both this law of levirate marriage and the story of Judah and Tamar show that widows were understood to have a strong interest in asserting their right to re-marry. Neither the story of Judah and Tamar, nor the law of levirate marriage, intimates that women were expected simply to defer to men who neglected their interests or rights.

The Book of Deuteronomy includes two other laws explicitly providing for women to appear in court—before "the elders at the gate." Both concern wives who also were mothers. The first of these is the ungovernable son statute in Deuteronomy 21:18–21. The NRSV translates the pertinent part as follows: "If someone has a stubborn and rebellious son, who will not obey his father and mother, who does not heed them when they discipline him, then his father and his mother shall take hold of him and

---

tiff in the local court and carried out the symbolic legal acts against the obstinate *levir*. In this case the widow defended her own right and not that of her deceased husband."

7. See the story of Ruth and Naomi, considered above in chapter 4, and below in chapter 11.

bring him out to the elders of his town at the gate of that place. They shall say to the elders of his town, 'This son of ours is stubborn and rebellious. He will not obey us. He is a glutton and a drunkard.'" According to this law, both the mother and the father are to testify, though perhaps not necessarily by reciting the words quoted here as to gluttony and dipsomania, which may be merely illustrative as to "stubborn and rebellious" conduct. It is significant that *both* parents were to present testimony, and that the elders were expected to credit the testimony of *both*.[8] This requirement accords with the two-witness law set out in Deuteronomy 19:15: "A single witness shall not prevail against a man[9] for any crime or for any wrong in connection with any offense that he has committed; only on the evidence of two witnesses, or of three witnesses, shall a charge be sustained." In this kind of case, both the father and mother were to testify as witnesses. This law clearly authorizes women to appear in court and testify as witnesses.

The other law where both parents were supposed to appear in court, found at Deuteronomy 22:13–21, concerns "tokens of virginity." When a newly married man claims that he "did not find in [his bride] the tokens of virginity," presumably during or just after the wedding night, the matter then may go to trial before the "elders of the city in the gate." The young woman's father, together with her mother, were to bring the physical evidence—*viz.*, the garment or bedclothes—before the elders. Having produced "the tokens of virginity," the father would then proceed to protest his daughter's innocence, after which he—evidently along with her mother—would "spread the garment before the elders of the city."[10] The elders would then "take the man and whip him" and "fine him a hundred

---

8. Compare Falk, *Law and Religion*, 80 ("The [father] is asked to submit his grievance to a judicial tribunal rather than to exercise his *ius vitae necisque* and the *patria potestas*"). It is unlikely that the biblical community would have been familiar with Latin expressions or Roman law when the laws of Deuteronomy were set down. Compare Boecker, *Law and Administration*, 30: "This text shows that the concept of family justice which gave the paterfamilias sovereign power over the members of the family had disappeared by the time Deuteronomy was written." See generally, Pressler, *View of Women*, 17–20.

9. The NRSV plausibly translates "person" rather than "man." See Sus vv. 34–40, where the two depraved elders testify against Susanna.

10. According to Deut 22:17: "*They* shall spread the garment before the elders . . ." emphasis supplied. The parents would be strongly motivated to find the requisite tokens, since absent such "tokens," their daughter would be stoned to death. In such circumstances, the story of Joseph and his brothers might suggest the possibility of producing blood stains from some other source. See Gen 37:29–33. So also Frymer-Kensky, "Virginity," 93–95, and same author, *Reading Women*, 172.

shekels of silver."[11] In this situation, the mother would appear, but not necessarily address the court other than by joining her husband in presenting the dispositive evidence.

Another instance of women taking their case to court is found in Numbers 27:1–11. Here, Mahlah, Noah, Hoglah, Milcah, and Tirzah—the five daughters of Zelophehad—"drew near" and "stood before Moses," other "leaders," and "all the congregation at the door of the tent of meeting," asking to be given the inheritance of their father. Moses "brought their case before YHWH," who then ruled in favor of the five sisters' petition, and Moses so decreed.[12] Later, the five sisters again appear in court, this time to seek enforcement of Moses' decree (Josh 17:3–6). There was no question in either narrative as to whether the sisters had the legal capacity to bring their case to court.

For the relatively brief period during which Israel and Judah were united as a single kingdom, the monarchy itself became a court—the highest court of the land. There being no separation of powers, the king would sit as judge or chief judge.[13] As an example, David was sitting in that capacity when Nathan came before him with the story about the rich man, the poor man, and the latter's pet lamb, causing David to pronounce judgment against himself in regard to the Bathsheba-Uriah episodes.[14] On another occasion, Joab, who was David's chief general and political advisor, arranged to send a woman ("the woman of Tekoa") before him with a "case" and a petition for judicial action (2 Sam 14:1–17). David had been mourning for his son, Absalom, who had recently murdered Amnon, his older brother. Absalom was in voluntary exile, and David had become morose and ineffectual. Joab put words in the woman's mouth, which, when spoken before David, prompted him to permit Absalom to

---

11. See Westbrook and Wells, *Everyday Law*, 84–85, suggesting that this law might have been in conflict with the law set out in Deut 19:16–21 which provides that those who offer malicious, false testimony be subjected to the same punishment as would be inflicted on the person falsely accused had the testimony been true. See above, chapter 7. Perhaps this law would apply in "tokens of virginity" cases if the new husband's testimony was found to be *intentionally and maliciously* false. But as written, there seems to be no conflict between the two laws. See also Pressler, *View of Women*, 22–31 (suggesting that the text can be read to mean that the woman's parents could sue the accusing husband for defamation and recover damages).

12. As to women inheriting property, see below chapter 11.

13. See Ps 72:1–4, 12–14, as to the king functioning as judge. See generally, Boecker, *Law and Administration*, 40–49.

14. 2 Sam 12:1–15. See chapter 2, above.

return from exile.[15] For present purposes, the point of interest is that there was no question whether the woman of Tekoa might address the court. She simply came to the king and proceeded to do so.[16]

The classic instance of women coming before the king in his judicial role involves Solomon and the two harlots or prostitutes, each claiming to be the mother of the one living child (1 Kgs 3:16–28). According to the story, the two women simply "came to the king and stood before him" and told their respective versions of the facts, each claiming that the live child was hers, and the dead child the other's. When Solomon proposes to settle the dispute by dividing the live child in two with a sword and giving half to each claimant, the true mother protests: "Oh, my lord, give her the living child, and by no means slay it," while the false claimant would rather the king gave each woman half of a dead child. The account, intended to illustrate Solomon's wisdom, clearly portrayed him in his judicial capacity: "And all Israel heard of the judgment which the king had rendered; and they stood in awe of the king, because they perceived that the wisdom of God was in him, to render justice" (1 Kgs 3:28). The text gives no indication that the women hesitated before coming before the court or that they acted against law or tradition when they did so.

Another woman, the Shunammite, whose story is told in 2 Kings 8:1–6 as part of the Elisha cycle, likewise appeals to "the king" for the return of her house and land.[17] Like Naomi and her family, this woman had been away for many years during a time of famine. While she was gone, someone took over her property. The king ruled in her favor, and even ordered restoration of "the produce of [her] fields from the day that she left the land until now" (2 Kgs 8:6).[18] Again, there is no suggestion that she acted contrary to law or common practice in asking the royal court for relief.

15. Whether David was wise in doing so is another question. A few years later, Absalom attempted to overthrow David, his father, and become king himself. As to the particulars, see Carmody, *Biblical Woman*, 44–48, and Hiers, *Justice and Compassion*, 66–67.

16. See 2 Sam 14:4: "When the woman of Tekoa came to the king, she fell on her face to the ground, and did obeisance, and said, 'Help, O king.'"

17. Also discussed below, chapter 9, note 5 and accompanying text.

18. Compare Boecker, *Law and Administration*, 51–52. Boecker suggests that the woman went to the king—not asking for judicial relief, but for him to give it back, because it was he who had taken over her property. Nothing in the text suggests that he had done so.

In the New Testament, Jesus tells a story, or parable, about a woman who—like the two women in the Solomon story and the Shunammite—went to court on their own initiative:

> He said, "In a certain city there was a judge who neither feared God nor regarded man; and there was a widow in that city who kept coming to him and saying, 'Vindicate me against my adversary.' For a while he refused; but afterward he said to himself, 'Though I neither fear God nor regard man, yet because this widow bothers me, I will vindicate her, or she will wear me out by her continual coming.'" (Luke 18:2–5)

Here again, there is no suggestion that such a woman would not have been admitted to court or the judge's presence. The behavior of this "unjust judge," contrasts with the responsiveness of "the Lord" as described in Sirach 35:13–15:

> He will not show partiality in the case of a poor man;
>   and he will listen to the prayer of one who is wronged.
> He will not ignore the supplication of the fatherless,
>   nor the widow when she pours out her story.
> Do not the tears of the widow run down her cheek
>   as she cries out against him who caused them to fall?

Both the parable and the saying in Sirach[19] imply that human judges should respond to the pleas of those who come before them—including women—by doing justice.

These several texts make it clear that in biblical times it was assumed that women could appear in court. There are no legal or narrative texts saying that they were barred from doing so. But were women understood to have the capacity to make contracts? And, related to that, might women in biblical times purchase, own, and sell property?

---

19. The text refers to God ("the Lord") as judge; but it is likely that the writer intended human judges to understand that they were expected to follow his example.

9

Capacity to Make Contracts and to Purchase, Own, and Sell Property

> The strong woman in [Proverbs] 31:10–31 owns a house and conducts her own business.
>
> —Silvia Schroer

ONE BIBLICAL TEXT EXPLICITLY refers to a woman signing a contract. This is in the late-biblical book of Tobit. Midway through the story, Tobit's son, Tobias wished to marry his cousin or near relative,[1] Sarah, the daughter of Raguel and Edna. Raguel proposes to delay the ceremony at least long enough for them all to "Eat, drink, and be merry"; but Tobias insists on their getting on with it:

> Tobias said, "I will eat nothing here until you make a binding agreement with me." So Raguel said, "Take her right now, in accordance with the law. You are her relative and she is yours. The merciful God will guide you both for the best." Then he called his daughter Sarah, and taking her by the hand he gave her to Tobias to be his wife, saying, "Here she is; take her according to the law of Moses, and take her with you to your father." And he blessed them. Next he called his wife Edna, and took out a scroll and wrote out the contract; and they set their seals to it. Then they began to eat. (Tob 7:9, 11–15)

Setting seals to a contract was equivalent to signing it; and even in modern times, seals are sometimes affixed to contracts and other documents.[2]

---

1. Tob 6:9–17. Other features of the book of Tobit have been examined above in chapter 2, and will be considered further below in chapters 10 and 11.

2. See Corbin, *Corbin on Contracts*, 337–44.

The fact that Edna had her own seal indicates that she was understood to have had the legal capacity to apply it to other written legal agreements as well. The detail is mentioned casually, as if it were nothing extraordinary. It can reasonably be assumed that, at least in the late-biblical period, other women also were recognized as having legal capacity to sign or set their seals to contracts.

Another text refers to a woman buying property. Such transactions necessarily involved agreements, whether oral or written, in the nature of contracts. Thus, among the attributes of the "good wife" described in Proverbs 31: "She considers a field and buys it" (Prov 31:16). Nothing in the text suggests that she was doing anything extraordinary, or that readers would be surprised by her considering and buying land. Evidently women were deemed legally capable with respect to buying property. Several other texts indicate that women owned houses in biblical times.

The book of Joshua states repeatedly that Rahab lived in her own house.[3] Although Rahab was a foreigner, and would have held title to her house under foreign, perhaps Canaanite law, there is no suggestion in these texts that it was unusual for a woman to own a house.[4] In the story of Ruth, it is said that after Naomi's husband and her two sons had died in the land of Moab, she urged her daughters-in-law, Orpah and Ruth, "Go, return each of you to her mother's house" (Ruth 1:8). Later, in the book of Ruth, it is said that Naomi was selling some land (Ruth 4:3–5), the obvious implication was that she then owned it. Several other texts mention, again incidentally, that various Israelite or Jewish women lived in their own house or owned property, as if women owning houses was commonplace. After having been raped by David, Bathsheba "returned to her house" (2 Sam 11:4). First Kings 17:1–24 records the story of Elijah's sojourning in a widow's house. Later, in 2 Kings 4:1–7, another story recounts Elisha's visiting the house of a widow and supplying her with oil for her to sell so that she could pay her debts. A married woman, the Shunammite—who figures in narratives at 2 Kings 4:8–37 and 8:1–6—is said to have been wealthy in her own right, and owner of "house," "land," and "fields."[5] The

---

3. Josh 2:1, 3, 15, 18, 19; 6:22.

4. Starr also draws attention to Josh 15:18–19, where a woman named Achsah is given a field with springs of water. *Bible Status*, 99. This text is repeated in Judg 1:14–15.

5. Compare Frymer-Kensky, "Bible and Women's Studies," 21: "The pronouns used are striking: *her* property? *her* farm? This is not the language we expect from the Bible, for the laws indicate that women did not own land. Surely, the land is her husband's, if he is still alive, or her son's." Frymer-Kensky does not identify any laws that preclude

"wanton woman" of Proverbs 9:13–18 "sits at the door of her house" and entertains "her guests" there. Proverbs 15:25 assured readers: "YHWH tears down the house of the proud, but maintains the widow's boundaries." In Proverbs 31:15, it is said that the good wife "provides food for her household."[6] The female lover in the Song of Solomon wishes that she could bring her friend "into the house of my mother" (Song 8:2). Micah 2:9 condemns those who drive women "out of their pleasant houses." And in the later biblical period, there is the story about Judith, a widow who had been left a considerable estate by her husband—which estate she, herself, maintained (Jdt 8:1–7).[7] The New Testament also includes references to widows' houses.[8] It can be said with some certainty that in biblical times, women were understood to have legal capacity to own houses and other property.

It appears that, at least in late biblical times, a man might decide to transfer his property, during his lifetime, to other persons, including his wife. That clearly is the implication of Sirach 33:19–23, where the Sage cautions:

> To a son or wife, to a brother or friend,
>   do not give power over yourself, as long as you live;
> and do not give your property to another,
>   lest you change your mind and must ask for it.
> While you are still alive and have breath in you,
>   do not let any one take your place.
> For it is better that your children should ask from you
>   than that you should look to the hand of your sons . . .
> At the time when you end the days of your life,
>   In the hour of death, distribute your inheritance.

It is not entirely clear whether the practice referred to here involved transferring property ownership or granting what in modern law is called a

---

women from owning land, nor does she comment on the many other texts indicating that women owned property. Elsewhere she suggests that the Shunammite owned the land by inheriting it, after the manner of the daughters of Zelophehad. *Reading Women*, 71–72. See below, chapter 10.

6. See Schroer, "Feminist Reconstruction," 140: "The strong woman in [Prov] 31:10–31 owns a house and conducts her own business." Schroer also points to Prov14:1 [Heb. text]: "[T]he wisdom of women builds her house" (NRSV).

7. See also Jdt 16:23–24. These texts are discussed below in chapter 10.

8. Mark 12:38–40; Luke 20:46–47. See also Luke 8:3 and Acts 12:12, referring to women who owned property.

"power of attorney" that would authorize the grantee, acting as a fiduciary, to make legally binding decisions on behalf of the grantor; in effect, to exercise the grantor's legal capacity. The Sage definitely disapproves of this practice; but the fact that he does so, indicates that he was aware that in his time people sometimes did transfer property or grant their power of attorney to family members or friends. Mention of "wife" shows that sometimes men might give their property, or "power" over themselves, to their wives. Such transfers of property or power probably were considered legally binding; otherwise the Sage's advice would have been unnecessary. Evidently women were understood to have legal capacity to take title to such property and to exercise such powers. The Sage recommends—for the reasons stated in the quoted text—that men wait to do so until they near the end of their days, in effect, by making a deathbed will or bequest.[9] The topic of transferring property by will or bequest is considered in the following chapter.

These several texts indicate that in the Old Testament period women might and often did own property. They could have purchased it or it could have been bequeathed to them or it could have been transferred to them by their husbands as inter-vivos gifts. Were women also understood to have legal capacity to sell property? According to the Book of Ruth, the answer is yes. Here we find Boaz negotiating with the *go'el* for the right to marry "the widow," meaning, in Boaz' mind, Ruth. Boaz begins by telling the *go'el*, "Naomi, who has come back from the country of Moab, is selling the parcel of land which belonged to our kinsman, Elimelech" (Ruth 4:3). How Ruth may have come into possession of "the parcel" will be considered later.[10] For present purposes, it is enough to observe that Boaz makes this statement as a matter of simple fact—as if there was no question whether Naomi was legally empowered to make the sale. Nor does the *go'el* express any misgivings as to this aspect of the negotiation. That Naomi had the right to sell the land is confirmed in two following verses, where Boaz refers to buying the land (or field) "from the hand of Naomi" (Ruth 4:5, 9). The sale itself would have involved an oral contract. Absent a court or office of written records, the transaction was carried out in

9. That transferring property earlier could have problematic consequences is illustrated in the NT, in Jesus' parable of the Prodigal Son (Luke 15:11–32). Here as in the background of Sir 33:19–23, it appears that such transfers were considered legal and binding, probably under common law.

10. See below, chapter 11.

the presence of witnesses (Ruth 4:4, 9–11). There being no indication to the contrary elsewhere in the Bible, it seems reasonable to conclude that other women likewise had the right or legal capacity to sell property.

The texts examined in this chapter suggest that in biblical times women could make legally binding contracts. Additionally, they could buy, own, and also sell property in their own name or right. In most of these instances, the women who owned property were widows. It is likely that in many cases, these properties would either have been left them as bequests by their husband, or inherited by them following their husband's deaths. Under certain circumstances, daughters, also, might own property that they had either inherited, or that had been bequeathed to them by their fathers. Relevant texts are considered in the next two chapters.

Biblical scholars generally do not distinguish between the transfer of property by will or bequest, and its transfer by inheritance through the "operation of law," namely, what in modern law is called the "law (or laws) of intestate succession." As will be seen in the two chapters that follow, this distinction appears in both biblical laws and biblical narratives. We turn first to wills or bequests where women were the designated beneficiaries.

10

Women as Beneficiaries of Wills
and Donors of Estates

And in all the land there were no women so fair as Job's daughters;
and their father gave them an inheritance among their brothers.

—Job 42:15

SEVERAL BIBLICAL NARRATIVES DESCRIBE procedures by which persons, usually men, transferred property to others in anticipation of their demise.[1] Some of these "gratuitous transfers"[2] could be characterized as wills or bequests. The book of Judith reports such a bequest: "[Judith's] husband Manasseh had left her gold and silver, and men and women slaves, and cattle, and fields; and she maintained this estate" (Jdt 8:7). She also inherited her husband's house,[3] though whether as part of his bequest, or under the common law of intestate succession,[4] is not specified.

Judith was not simply the beneficiary of her husband's estate. At the end of the story, she bequeathed her estate to both her husband's and to her own heirs: "Before she died she distributed *her property* to all those who were next of kin to her husband Manasseh, and to her own nearest

---

1. See Westbrook and Wells, *Everyday Law*, 101–4; and Hiers, "Transfer of Property," 147–52.

2. In modern estate and trusts jurisprudence, the term "gratuitous transfer" refers to the gift or transfer of property from one person to another when there is no payment or tangible consideration in exchange for the gift.

3. See Jdt 8:4–5 referring to her living "at home as a widow," and "her house." See also Jdt 16:23: "She . . . grew old in her husband's house, until she was a hundred and five years old."

4. See below, chapter 11.

kindred" (Jdt 16:24).[5] Evidently the estate was hers to distribute as she saw fit. Presumably other women had the right or capacity to bequeath property, at least in the latter part of the biblical period.

The book of Job ends with another reported bequest. Here it is said that Job left his estate not only to his seven (unnamed) sons, but also to his three daughters, Jemimah, Keziah, and Kerenhappuch: "[T]heir father gave them an inheritance along with their brothers" (Job 42:13–15, NRSV). It may be inferred that the narrator intended to represent Job's doing so as further evidence of his having lived a righteous life. Here "inheritance" (Heb.: *nachalah*) refers to a share of the estate. It might be assumed that Job's sons and daughters received equal shares; but that is not specified.

In both the Book of Judith and the story of Job, women came into possession of property through bequests: in one case from a husband, in the other from their father. These stories may indicate that others also in biblical times occasionally bequeathed some or all of their estates to wives or daughters. At any rate, the stories may have been intended to suggest that readers consider doing so as well.

Several biblical narratives describe wills or bequests in which other persons were the beneficiaries.[6] One notable example is in the story of Tobit, where Raguel, the donor, states that the estate in question would pass to Tobias, the beneficiary, after both he *and his wife* die (Tob 8:20–21). Here it seems to be assumed that if Raguel pre-deceased his wife, the estate would first pass to her, and only then after her death to the named beneficiary.[7] It is possible, though unlikely, that Raguel and his wife, Edna, owned their property in common under some arrangement such as what now is referred to as "joint tenancy with right of survivorship." In that case, the arrangement would have had the same legal effect as a will or bequest to the surviving spouse. Or each may have made a will leaving their respective shares in the estate to the other. It appears more likely, however, that at the demise of whichever spouse died first,

5. Emphasis added. She also "set her maid free." Jdt 16:23. It is not said that she emancipated other slaves.

6. See Hiers, *Justice and Compassion*, 52–56.

7. See also Tob 14:13, where, at the end of the story, it is said that after both Raguel and his wife died, Tobias inherited "*their* property." Emphasis supplied.

the entire estate would pass to the other by operation of law,[8] also known, in modern Anglo-American law, as the law or laws of intestate succession.

The biblical law of intestate succession spells out the circumstances under which daughters might inherit their father's property. Biblical tradition also includes a number of accounts where it appears that widows inherited property by operation of law. These will be considered in the following chapter.

8. See further discussion of Raguel's and Edna's estate in the next chapter.

11

Women as Heirs to Property
by Operation of Law

[W]e must admit that the book of Ruth assumes the practice of
inheritance by widows . . . At any rate our author assumes that his
readers will not regard it as strange.

—Millar Burrows

L IKE MODERN ANGLO-AMERICAN LAW, biblical law distinguished between gratuitous transfers of property by a donor in prospect of his
or her death by making a will or bequest, and inheritance of property by
operation of law or "the laws of intestate succession."[1] Such laws identify
which heirs will inherit property in the event that the deceased had not so
designated by making a will or bequest during his or her lifetime.

   In early biblical times, the law or laws of intestate succession had
not yet been written down. Instead, succession probably was governed
by customary or "common law." Normally under such common law, it
seems that sons inherited their fathers' property, but daughters did not.[2]
In two different accounts the "daughters of Zelophehad" go to court
in order to argue that they should be given their father's inheritance.[3]
Zelophehad had five daughters but no sons. The question presented was
one of "first impression," since none of the earlier biblical law codes had
specified what should be done under such circumstances. The daughters

1. See generally, Hiers, "Transfer of Property."
2. However, in some ancient Near Eastern societies, daughters could sometimes be
heirs. See Westbrook and Wells, *Everyday Law*, 93.
3. Num 27:1–11; Josh 17:3–6, discussed above, chapter 8, text accompanying note 12.
The daughters are named in both accounts: Mahlah, Noah, Hoglah, Milcah, and Tirzah.

appealed to Moses, who brought the matter "before YHWH," and YHWH then set out what was to become the only written biblical law of intestate succession:

> The daughters of Zelophehad are right; you shall give them possession of an inheritance among their father's brethren and cause the inheritance of their father to pass to them. And you shall say to the people of Israel, "If a man dies, and has no son, then you shall cause his inheritance to pass to his daughter. And if he has no daughter, then you shall give his inheritance to his brothers. And if he has no brothers, then you shall give his inheritance to his father's brothers. And if his father has no brothers, then you shall give his inheritance to his kinsman that is next to him of his family, and he shall possess it. And it shall be to the people of Israel a statute and ordinance, as YHWH commanded Moses." (Num 27:5–11)

It is noteworthy that, in the absence of a son or sons, the deceased's daughter or daughters had precedence over all his male relatives.[4] To the extent that daughters did not inherit if they had brothers, the law or common law of intestate succession was not applied evenly.[5] On the other hand, daughters might be given substantial dowries out of their parents' property. Such dowries could include land.[6]

This law of intestate succession makes no mention of widows. And yet biblical tradition reports several instances where widows occupied and apparently held title to property that previously belonged to their deceased husbands. Moreover, as has been seen in previous chapters, a wife might own property and obtain title to property by gratuitous transfer either during her husband's lifetime or as beneficiary of his will. The question then is, if a husband died without making a will, did his widow inherit his property by operation of law?

The first account where a widow evidently inherited her deceased husband's property is found in the book of Ruth. The story begins with

---

4. However, this law does not include sisters or aunts as possible heirs.

5. A later law referring to the daughters of Zelophehad and women similarly situated, specifies that such heiresses might not marry outside "the family of the tribe of their fathers," lest the inheritances of one tribe be transferred to persons of another tribe. See Num 36:1–9. Whether the Num 36 law was ever enforced (or enforceable) is another matter. Some such law is alluded to in Tob 4:12–13, and 6:9–12, but does not come into play elsewhere in biblical tradition.

6. See Westbrook and Wells, *Everyday Law*, 98–101.

a short summary of the family situation. A man named Elimelech was married to Naomi, and the couple had two sons, Mahlon and Chilion. In time of famine, all four moved from Judah to Moab. Soon afterwards, Elimelech died, and later the sons married young Moabite women, respectively, Ruth and Orpah. The five surviving members of the family continued to live in Moab for several years, but then both Mahlon and Chilion died without having any children. Naomi now plans to return to Judah, but encourages her two daughters-in-law to remain in Moab and find new husbands for themselves there. Orpah reluctantly agrees to stay in Moab, but Ruth insists on going along with Naomi.

The two women come to Bethlehem and make their home there.[7] Presumably this home belonged to Naomi, for later in the narrative, she undertakes to help Ruth find a home of her own (Ruth 3:1). Naomi's house in Bethlehem probably was the same one where she and Elimelech and their sons had lived before moving to Moab. If so, it would appear that Naomi had inherited this home from her deceased husband.

Naomi evidently owned some additional property that is said to have belonged to Elimelech, namely, agricultural land, also referred to as a "field." Or so, Boaz, their relative, says in the course of his negotiation with the nearer kinsman (or *go'el*) as to who should "redeem" it.[8] The following extended quotation contains a number of clues:

> And Boaz went up to the gate and sat down there; and behold, the next of kin, of whom Boaz had spoken, came by. So Boaz said, "Turn aside, friend; sit down here"; and he turned aside and sat down. And he took ten men of the elders of the city, and said, "Sit down here"; so they sat down. Then he said to the next of kin, "Naomi, who has come back from the country of Moab, is selling the parcel of land which belonged to our kinsman Elimelech. So I thought I would tell you of it, and say, Buy it in the presence of those sitting here, and in the presence of the elders of my people. If you will redeem it, redeem it; but if you will not, tell me, that I may know, for there is no one besides you to redeem it, and I come after you." And he said, "I will redeem it." Then Boaz said, "The day you buy the field from the hand of Naomi, you are also buying

7. Presumably they did not live on the street, and nothing is said about their staying with friends or relations. As will be noted, other widows lived in houses most likely inherited from their husbands.

8. As to redemption of land in ancient Israel, see Lev 25:25 and Westbrook and Wells, *Everyday Law*, 122.

Ruth the Moabitess,[9] the widow of the dead, in order to restore the name of the dead to his inheritance." Then the next of kin said, "I cannot redeem it for myself, lest I impair my own inheritance. Take my right of redemption yourself, for I cannot redeem it." . . .

So when the next of kin said to Boaz, "Buy it for yourself," he drew off his sandal. Then Boaz said to the elders and all the people, "You are witnesses this day that I have bought from the hand of Naomi all that belonged to Elimelech and all that belonged to Chilion and to Mahlon. Also Ruth the Moabitess, the widow of Mahlon, I have bought to be my wife, to perpetuate the name of the dead in his inheritance, that the name of the dead may not be cut off from among his brethren and from the gate of his native place; you are witnesses this day." Then all the people who were at the gate, and the elders, said, "We are witnesses." (Ruth 4:1–11a)

It may be noticed that prior to this scene, there had been no mention of Naomi's having intended to sell the field. Linking buying (redeeming) the field with the obligation to marry the widow may have been part of Boaz' negotiating strategy. The idea that buying the land and marrying the widow was a package deal evidently caught the nearer kinsman by surprise. Boaz' contention seems to have been that if the nearer kinsman was going to act the part of the *goël* by redeeming the land (Lev 25:25), he would then also be obliged to marry the widow (Deut 25:5). The nearer kinsman did not challenge Boaz' interpretation of the law, but balked at the prospect of marrying "the widow" and so waived his status as *goël*.[10]

The "parcel of land" is said to have "belonged to" Elimelech; and Boaz advised the nearer kinsman that he would be buying it "from the hand of Naomi" (Ruth 4:5). Actually, however, according to the Hebrew text, the kinsman was told that he would be buying it "from the hand of" *both* Naomi and Ruth. If Ruth owned part of the land, it likely would have

9. But see the Hebrew text, translated and discussed by Daube, *Ancient Jewish Law*, 37–43: "What day you buy the field from the hand of Naomi and from Ruth the Moabitess, you have bought the wife of the dead to raise up the name of the dead upon his inheritance." Ibid., 39. So also the KJV translation. The Hebrew text thus leaves open the question which "widow" the nearer kinsman would have to marry. Daube proposes that Boaz meant to lead the nearer kinsman to believe it would be Naomi, and therefore decide to waive his right (or avoid his obligation) to marry "the widow," so that he, Boaz, could then go ahead and marry Ruth.

10. Boaz may have "reached" to combine the two roles. Leviticus 25:25 applied only when the property had already been sold; and in its terms, Deut 25:5–10 refers only to the obligation of the deceased's *brother*, and then only if the brothers had "dwelled together."

been understood that she had acquired it by inheritance from Mahlon, her husband, upon his death. Here is further evidence that widows inherited their husbands' property. However, a few verses later, Boaz declares that he bought "from the hand of Naomi all that belonged to Elimelech and all that belonged to Chilion and to Mahlon" (Ruth 4:9).[11] Possibly the narrator or an early copyist simply omitted the previous phrase, "and from Ruth"; or it could be that Boaz or the narrator understood that Naomi was acting for both herself and Ruth.

It also is possible that on Elimelech's death, both of his two sons, who then were adults, had inherited some or all of his property. Naomi may or may not have inherited a "spousal share"—as so characterized in modern Anglo-American jurisprudence. Then, when Mahlon died, Ruth would have inherited his share, while after Chilion died, Naomi would have retained her spousal share, and/or inherited the share that had previously passed to Chilion, since Chilion's widow, who remained in Moab, effectively abandoned or renounced anything she would have inherited from him. Possibly under common law, title to any property deceased childless sons had inherited would have reverted back to their mother and/ or their own widows. It is unlikely that Naomi would have been holding the property in trust for her sons or any other progeny, since both sons were dead, and there was no expectation that she would have any more children to take title to it. In any case, if Naomi (and perhaps Ruth) had not inherited the land, one would have to ask who then did own it, and how it happened that Naomi came to be selling it.[12]

11. Boaz goes on to say that he had "bought" Ruth, the widow of Mahlon, "to perpetuate the name of the dead in his inheritance" (Ruth 4:10). By saying he had "bought" Ruth, Boaz evidently meant that he had undertaken to fulfill the obligations of levirate marriage, as set out somewhat differently in Deut 25:5–9. See Ruth 3:12 –13. There is no indication that Ruth was "for sale," or that Boaz paid anyone for marrying her. See Boecker, *Law and Administration*, 101, commenting on both Babylonian marriage in the time of Hammurabi and on marriage in the OT: "The term 'purchase' really refers to no more than the legal form for contracting the marriage." See also Levine, "Legal Themes," 101: "No notion of marriage as purchase may be imputed to the author of Ruth." See also Burrows, quoted above, chapter 5, note 40.

12. Thus Burrows, "Marriage of Boaz," 448: "[W]e must admit that the book of Ruth assumes the practice of inheritance by widows . . . At any rate our author assumes that his readers will not regard it as strange." Compare Frymer-Kensky, *Reading Women*, 246–52, suggesting, inter al., that Naomi did not own the land, but might have been selling "'land futures,' the right to redeem the land at some future time" (ibid., 250), or that Naomi (or Ruth) wanted Boaz to "reacquire Elimelekh's field from whoever now has it," after which Boaz would "have first right of purchase if Naomi then sells it" (ibid., 248). Also compare

Naomi may have wished to sell the "parcel of land" because she needed the money. If she sold it to someone outside the extended circle of relatives, its title would pass out of the family. But if she sold it to a kinsman, it would thereby be "redeemed," that is, kept in the family. If the nearer kinsman bought it as *goʾel*, he would have to return it to Naomi's heir or heirs. But Naomi had no heir or heirs—unless someone played the part of the levirate *goʾel* by marrying Ruth, her son's widow, so that she might have a grandson who could eventually inherit the property. Boaz was willing to play the part of the *goʾel* in both roles. Any child or children born to Boaz and Ruth would then, in time, inherit the land Boaz was purchasing from Naomi. It all may have been that simple.

For present purposes, however, it is unnecessary to sort out all the possibilities. Boaz's main purpose, as the story is told, was to persuade the nearer kinsman to renounce his right (or duty) to marry Ruth, since Boaz himself, wished to marry her, as is said plainly in Ruth 3:10–13. Those who heard or read the story in biblical times probably would have understood that Naomi had come into ownership of the property she was selling by inheriting it from her deceased husband—whether or not Ruth also had inherited part of the property from her husband, Mahlon.

The fact that the field in question had not passed directly to the deceased Elimilech's nearest male kinsman, is further evidence that widows inherited their husbands' property. According to the law of intestate succession considered above, if a man had no sons or daughters, brothers or uncles, his inheritance would pass to his nearest kinsman (Num 27:5–11). But that had not happened.[13] Instead, if the nearer kinsman or *goʾel* wished to acquire the field, he would have to *buy* it *from Naomi*. But he declined to do so. Nothing in the story suggests that those who first heard or read it would find this situation surprising. Apparently it was understood that the widow would inherit before all others, at least before (and instead of) her deceased husband's male kinsmen.

Several other biblical texts suggest that widows inherited property from their husbands.[14] In the story about Elijah's staying as a guest or tenant with the widow at Zarepthath,[15] it is said that he stayed with her

---

Sasson, *Ruth*, 108–15, suggesting that Naomi was in possession of the land, was selling it, and would be entitled to the proceeds of the sale, but had not inherited it.

13. See discussion by Levine, "Legal Themes," 102–3.

14. Compare ibid., 103: "Women did not inherit their husband's wealth in Israel."

15. 1 Kgs17:8–24.

in her house (1 Kgs 17:17, 23); that he provided food for her "household" for many days (1 Kgs 17:15); and took her ailing child into the "upper chamber" of this house, where he had his bed (1 Kgs 17:19–23). It is not said explicitly that this widow had inherited the house from her deceased husband; but this is the most likely explanation for her being there and apparently owning it. A somewhat similar story is told in 2 Kings 4:1–7, this time about the prophet Elisha and another widow. Here, the widow and her two children are living in a house, but are in debt. Elisha enables the widow and her children to pay off the debt by magically filling large numbers of vessels with oil for her to sell. Again, it is not said how it happened that the widow continued to be living in "the house," but the story teller evidently assumed that readers would understand that she had inherited it—along, perhaps, with the debt. In both of these stories, it may be significant that the widow's sons were minors; possibly not old enough to inherit or take title to their father's property.

The Shunammite woman, whose story is told in 2 Kings 4 and 8, also seems to have inherited property from her husband. In the earlier chapter, she is said to have been "a wealthy woman" with a living, though un-named husband. However in 2 Kings 8:1–6, which is set seven years later, there is no mention of her husband. It is reasonable to infer that he had died in the meantime. Now the narrator refers to "*her* house and *her* land" (2 Kgs 8:3).[16]

As in later times, unscrupulous relatives or neighbors may have been tempted to take advantage of widows by moving property lines or by fraudulent dealings of one kind or another. The book of Proverbs includes the following warning: "YHWH tears down the house of the proud, but maintains the widow's boundaries" (Prov 15:25). It seems likely that the property referred to by the term "widow's boundaries" would be land which the widows inherited from their husbands.

Several prophets condemned their contemporaries for oppressing widows. For instance:

> Woe to those who decree iniquitous decrees,
>   and the writers who keep writing oppression,
> to turn aside the needy from justice
>   and to rob the poor of my people of their right,

---

16. Emphasis supplied. See Burrows, *Outline*, 302: "Inheritance or at least trusteeship by a widow is presupposed by Ru. 4:3 and 2 K 8:1–6." Compare Frymer-Kensky, quoted above chapter 9, note 5.

that widows may be their spoil,
    and that they may make the fatherless their prey. (Isa 10:1–2)

"For if you truly amend your ways and your doings, if you truly ex-
ecute justice one with another, if you do not oppress the alien, the
fatherless or the widow, . . . then I will let you dwell in this place,
in the land that I gave of old to your fathers for ever." (Jer 7:5–7)

Woe to those who devise wickedness
    and work evil upon their beds!
When the morning dawns, they perform it,
    because it is in the power of their hand.
They covet fields, and seize them;
    and houses, and take them away;
they oppress a man and his house,
    a man and his inheritance . . .
The women of my people you drive out
    from their pleasant houses . . . (Mic 2:1–9)[17]

The women's "pleasant houses" referred to evidently would have been
part of their husbands' "inheritance."

The story of Tobit also suggests that widows inherited from their
husbands. Raguel and his wife, Edna, had already put their seals to a pre-
nuptial contract of some sort.[18] Now, toward the end of the subsequent
fourteen-day wedding feast, Raguel "declared by oath" that after the feast
was over, Tobias, their daughter, Sarah's new husband, "should take half
of Raguel's property and return in safety to his father, and that the rest
would be his 'when my wife and I die'" (Tob 8:19–21). The last clause can
be read to imply that whether Raguel or his wife Edna dies first, the other
would inherit the rest of "the rest," that is the other half of the property
they had retained, before this property would pass to Tobias.[19] Even if

17. As to oppression of widows and other vulnerable members of the community,
see, e.g., Exod 22:21–24; Jer 5:26–28; 9:4–6; 22:3; Amos 2:6–8; 4:1; 5:11–12; 8:4–6; and
Mic 3:1–3.

18. Tob 7:13–14. See above, chapter 9.

19. One might speculate whether, if Sarah had not married, she would have inherited
her parents' estate. Absent any brothers, that would have been the case under the law of
the "daughters of Zelophehad." But since she did marry, it seems here that her husband
would inherit the estate. Or it may be that Raguel's oath was in effect an oral contract or
a will, setting out the conditions under which Tobias would inherit property belonging
to Sarah's parents.

Raguel and Edna owned this retained property jointly, whichever of them survived the other evidently would have inherited the other's share. This meaning is confirmed by the fact that at the end of the story, it is said that Tobias inherited "their property," that is, the property that had belonged to both his father-in-law, and his mother-in-law (Tob 14:13).

And in the New Testament, Jesus is said to have warned his hearers not to be taken in by seemingly pious scribes (or lawyers) "who like to go about in long robes, and to have salutations in the market places and the best seats in the synagogues and the places of honor at feasts, who devour widow's houses and for a pretense make long prayers" (Mark 12:38–40).[20] It is reasonable to assume that such widows were understood to have inherited their husbands' houses.

It seems unlikely that *all* of the widows discussed in this chapter who owned property had inherited it as daughters of Zelophehad, or like Job's daughters, as beneficiaries of parental bequests. Instead, the instances considered here reasonably lead to the conclusion that, in biblical times, wives inherited their deceased husbands' property, even though there is no provision for their doing so in the written law of intestate succession. That widows might so inherit could have been customary practice under common law.[21] If so, there would have been no need to include widows in the law promulgated in response to the petition by the daughters of Zelophehad (Num 27:5–11). This law, the only written biblical law of intestate succession, was set down for the sole purpose of establishing what would happen if a father died with daughters, but with no sons to inherit. There is no mention of Zelophehad's widow, who presumably had died, and the question whether widows inherit was not presented in the case.

That wives died before their husbands may well have been commonplace, especially given the absence of modern obstetrical care. For instance, Abraham's wife, Sarah, pre-deceased him, and Rachel died (in childbirth) before Jacob. In the New Testament, Jesus' saying in response to the two brothers who wished him to adjudicate their claims to inheritance makes no mention of their mother (Luke 12:13); nor does the parable of the Prodigal Son (Luke 15:11–32), which likewise involves the

20. See also Luke 20:46–47, a parallel or duplicate version of the same saying.

21. See Westbrook and Wells, *Everyday Law*, 101: "Some Near Eastern law codes provide for the widow to receive a share of her late husband's estate, at least for her lifetime." Although biblical law codes do not so provide, common law, represented in these ancient Near Eastern codes, may have been applied in the biblical instances discussed here.

allocation of inherited property between surviving brothers. There are no instances in biblical narratives where it is said that either sons or daughters inherited their father's property while the deceased's widow was still alive.[22]

In any case, there are no biblical instances where sons of any age inherited *instead of* the deceased's widow. It appears therefore that in biblical times, a surviving widow normally inherited her deceased husbands' estate. Thus it may be concluded that under the unwritten or common law of intestate succession, widows were first in line to inherit their husbands' property.

22. In some instances considered above, widows with young or minor children evidently inherited their husbands' property. Whether they held that property in trust until such children came of age is certainly possible, but there are no textual indications one way or the other. The story of Ruth suggests that after Elimelech's death, Naomi's adult sons, Mahlon and Chilion, *might have* inherited some of their father's property even though their mother, Naomi, was still alive. It is also possible that Elimelech had transferred the "field" in question, or portions of it, to his sons either before his death, or by bequest. In any case, the fact that Naomi was *selling* the "parcel of land" indicates that it was hers; and since it had previously belonged to her husband (Ruth 4:3), the most likely way it would have come to her was by inheritance, whether from her husband, one or both of her sons, or from all three of the deceased.

12

Summary of Findings

WOMEN IN OLD TESTAMENT times evidently enjoyed many of the same legal rights and protections as did men.[1] That such should have been the case ought not be surprising, given the largely affirmative attitudes regarding women found in the cultural milieu that comes to expression throughout the Old Testament. As in other societies, culturally shared values usually provide the foundation for the legal system.

Virtually all biblical accounts of relations between husbands—including the so-called "patriarchs"—and their wives represent the wives as strong and independent persons.[2] Contrary to what might be expected from YHWH-God's words to the first woman as told in Genesis 3:16—"[Y]our desire shall be for your husband, and he shall rule over you"—no Old Testament narrative includes a scene in which a man rules over his wife.[3] Instead, Old Testament wives evidently felt free to express their own views or take decisive actions, sometimes in opposition to their husbands' wishes or desires. Notable examples include: Sarah, Rebekah, Rachel, Abigail, Michal, Bathsheba, Jezebel, Vashti, Esther, and Anna, the wife of Tobit. There are no meek or obsequious wives—or other such women—in the Old Testament.

Biblical tradition records a number of stories—albeit some probably legendary—about women who were remembered for important deeds

---

1. Compare Bird, "Images of Women," 56: "The picture of woman obtained from the Old Testament laws can be summarized in the first instance as that of a legal non-person ... The laws, by and large, do not address her; most do not even acknowledge her existence."

2. See Frymer-Kensky, *Reading Women*, 333: "The women who appear in biblical stories are often striking characters, distinct personalities ..."

3. See above, chapters 1 and 2.

in critical times. Among these, particularly: Rahab, Deborah, Ja'el, and Judith. Several other women were remembered for acting boldly when occasion arose. A few women were recognized as prophets: Deborah, again, and also Miriam—both celebrated also for the "songs" attributed to them—as well as Huldah, among others. Four women played major leadership roles: Deborah, as judge, as well as commander-in-chief over Israel's fighting forces; Jezebel and Athaliah, as queens, respectively, of Israel and Judah; and Judith, who personally seduced, then decapitated the enemy general, Holofernes, and set in motion the defeat of his mighty army. Biblical books or writings are named for four women: Ruth, Esther, Judith, and Susanna, thereby commemorated for their respective significant roles or merits.

Women are generally seen as powerful and important people in many Old Testament writings. In positive terms, the first woman, like the first man, was said to have been made "in the image of God." One late biblical narrator even insists that men ought to appreciate the fact that women "rule over" them. On the other hand, one of the wisdom writers considered women so deleteriously potent that they are to blame for shame, sin, disgrace and death. Several proverbs warn simple men against the peril of intimacy with "loose" or seductive women.

Many passages in both laws and wisdom writings, accord mothers the same measure of respect and deference that was due to fathers. Daughters seem to have been regarded with affection, even though those who were "impudent" or "headstrong" could cause their fathers anxiety and grief. Wisdom writers view a wise, good, prudent, intelligent, and loyal wife as a man's greatest blessing; while a contentious (or "brawling") wife could drive her husband to distraction—if not out of the house. Several laws as well as other Old Testament texts called on people in the community to protect widows from oppression, and established a variety of arrangements to assure their continuing welfare.

In view of a remembered history in which women played prominent leadership roles—one even sitting as judge in her judicial capacity—and the importance of women as members of and participants in the ongoing community, it would have been strange if women were not regarded as persons with legal status, and more specifically, with legal capacity. Examination of relevant texts leads to the conclusion that in biblical times, women were so recognized.

Although there is little mention of specific rights, several laws clearly established obligations on the part of others in the community. The corollary implicit in these laws is that the women affected had the right to have these obligations enforced. Significantly, these obligations and rights all related to women in situations where they would have been especially vulnerable: widows, pregnant wives, daughters who had been sold as slaves or servants, and captive women taken as wives.

In several other kinds of situations, women were entitled to the same rights or protections as men. This was true not only of free persons, but also in the case of slaves. The term "equal protection," of course, is not found in the Bible; but the underlying belief that men and women were of equal value before God and entitled to equal standing before the law, was implicit in a number of biblical laws.[4] Some of these laws referred specifically to rights of, or protections for, female slaves.

Some scholars assume that in biblical times women were denied access to courts of law. However, no biblical law bars women from appearing in court, nor are there any reports of women being so barred. Three laws explicitly provide for women to come before "the elders at the gate," in effect, local courts. In one setting, women were to come to court in order to vindicate their own rights; in another, to prosecute offenders or act as witnesses; and in the third, to present evidence. Several biblical narratives involve women coming before the court, in one case, to exculpate herself before her accuser, and in others, to petition officials, sometimes the king (sitting as judge), to resolve disputes or rule on other legal questions. One of Jesus' parables likewise represents a woman seeking justice from a judge. It appears that in biblical times, women had the right to appear in court on their own behalf, both as witnesses, and as parties to disputes.

It also seems clear that women, like men, had the right to enter into contractual arrangements, whether oral or written, and to apply their own seals to legal documents. In this connection, women could buy or sell land. Many instances show that women could own land, houses, and other property. And—though there are only a few examples—women, like men, could be beneficiaries of wills or bequests. Moreover, women could make wills leaving their property to others.

---

4. The poor and immigrants (or sojourners) also constituted what might now be considered "protected classes." The same could be said regarding slaves, generally, although to a lesser degree. See Hiers, *Justice and Compassion*, 75–79.

Under the written law of intestate succession, a man's daughters might inherit his property, but only if the man had no sons. This arrangement clearly was disadvantageous to daughters who had brothers. However, the same law provided that, in the absence of brothers, such daughters would be in line to inherit ahead of all the deceased's surviving male relatives such as brothers, uncles, and all other kinsmen. The written law of intestate succession made no mention of widows.

The most surprising, and perhaps controversial, conclusion of this study is that, under the common law of intestate succession, when a married man died, his widow would be first in line to inherit his estate. Not only are there several instances where narratives refer to widows being in possession of their deceased husband's property; there are no instances where sons or other male relatives were said to have inherited property of the deceased when the deceased had a surviving widow.[5] This common law of intestate succession may have been based on early Israelite custom, or it may have been borrowed from common law deriving from legal decisions and practice in other ancient Near Eastern societies.

In summary, it appears that in biblical times, women were considered to be persons with a number of legal rights; that in many respects, the law treated women the same way it did men; that women had legal capacity to appear in court, to enter into contracts, to possess property, to be beneficiaries of wills and to make bequests; that in limited circumstances, daughters could inherit from their fathers; and that under common law of intestate succession, widows inherited from their deceased husbands.

5. See above, chapter 11, note 22, discussing a possible exception. Interpreters generally seem reluctant to recognize that widows could and did inherit their husband's property. See, e.g., Schroer, "Feminist Reconstruction," 123: "Since [widows] cannot inherit the land of their husbands, they are without means and depend on the benevolence of their relatives. Most often what they have left is the house and a small plot of land (see 2 Kings 8:3) . . ." Schroer does not explain why widows could not inherit their husband's land, or how widows, notwithstanding, might "often" have such property "left" if not by inheritance. Nor does she explain how the land referred to in 2 Kgs 8:3 became only "a small plot." Compare 2 Kgs 8:6.

13

As to Christian Ethics and Social Policy

THE OLD TESTAMENT IS one of the most influential collections of writings in the Western world and much of the rest of the world as well. It is the foundational scripture for Judaism and Christianity, and ancillary scripture for Islam. For most of the first two centuries CE, the Old Testament, in its Septuagint and other versions, was *the* Christian Bible. Through the centuries that followed, the Bible, now including the New Testament and what came to be called the Old Testament Apocrypha, was "the book" or "library" of books most commonly read by Christian and other people in Europe, North America, and many other countries and continents.

For centuries, beginning with paintings on the walls of early Christian and Jewish catacombs, biblical scenes have been favorite subjects in the graphic arts; Western literature abounds in allusions to Old Testament personalities, narratives, and sayings;[1] biblical tradition has contributed at least indirectly to the development of Western law;[2] and to the present time, many biblical texts and topics have been set to music—both popular and classical. Politicians continue to cite biblical texts as precedent and authority; and biblical texts have inspired major social movements, from medieval times, to anti-slavery efforts in the eighteenth and nineteenth centuries, to the "social gospel" of the late nineteenth and early twentieth centuries, the later civil rights movement of the 1950s and '60s, various liberation theologies, and contemporary concerns about poverty, hunger, health issues, nuclear weapons, wildlife and endangered species, climate change, and global warming.

1. See, e.g., Soelle, *Great Women*.
2. See, e.g., Berman, *Law and Revolution*.

Yet many people, including professing as well as nominal Christians, are surprisingly ignorant as to the contents of the Bible. And not only ignorant, but misinformed.[3] Those who were introduced to "Bible stories" in their Sunday school years may tend to assume that when they became adults, they outgrew the Bible, not realizing that the Bible was written for and by adults. Or that it relates to profound existential questions, such as the meaning of life, good and evil, right and wrong, justice and injustice, mortality, human hopes, fears, and responsibility for actions that affect other persons and other living things.[4] Such questions are not altogether different now than they were two or three thousand years—a mere hundred to a hundred and fifty generations—ago when the Bible was being written down.[5]

People often assume that, by virtue of its antiquity, (or perhaps because they consider its contents not only passé but also misguided), biblical tradition has nothing to say as to current human conditions. Readers of this present book, of course, will draw their own conclusions about these matters. Yet a few areas of interest stand out, particularly with respect to the relevance of biblical Old Testament tradition for Christian ethics and social ethics. Here we consider three sets of such interest. The first of these has to do with relations between husbands and wives. Another set of reflections has to do with the contrasting ideals of individualism and community welfare. A third concerns women's rights and what is now referred to as the equal protection of the laws.

3. Among many commonplace, and largely harmless instances: the ideas that in the book of Genesis Adam and Eve were told not to eat fruit from the "tree of knowledge"; that the fruit in question was "an apple"; that they were tempted to eat it by Satan; that Eve *made* her husband eat of it; and that the primordial pair were evicted from the Garden of Eden for engaging in improper sexual activity. Also, the traditional, but biblically unwarranted assumptions that Moses wrote the first five books of the Bible, David all the psalms, and Solomon all the proverbs. More potentially detrimental instances include the notions that by separating the sea from the dry land, God sanctioned racial segregation; that God cursed Ham and told him he would be a slave to his brothers, thereby legitimating enslaving persons of African ancestry; that the only *humans* created by God were white people, all others having been created as inferior beings of some sort; and that "the Bible" tells "us" that "we" should use up all the earth's resources before "the Lord" returns. Some possible misreadings and over- (or under-) interpretations of biblical texts relating to women's status and rights have been noted in this book.

4. See generally, Hiers, "Reverence for Life."

5. See Frymer-Kensky, *Reading Women*, 350–54, suggesting a number of ways biblical narratives can "make us question the perfection of our own society." Ibid., 351.

HUSBANDS AND WIVES

It cannot be said that biblical accounts portray exemplary democratic family life. Children were subject to parental authority—the authority of both parents—and parents' exercise of that authority could take severe forms. Yet stories describing relations between husbands and wives, typically, if not invariably, represent the latter—including the wives of the so-called patriarchs—as independent and determined personalities.[6] As has been seen, these women were quite capable of holding their own in family disputes and, at times, of acting against their husbands' expressed wishes. Nowhere in the Old Testament are wives said to be "property." Nor are any ever characterized as mere "housewives." With the sole exception of Genesis 3:16, biblical texts describing women as subordinate or subject to their husbands are found only in the New Testament. This fact might explain why such New Testament texts are particularly popular in some conservative religious circles where they can function to re-enforce existing cultural norms.[7] At any rate, acquaintance with the Old Testament's portrait gallery of strong-minded and self-assertive wives might encourage and empower latter-day wives who yearn to pursue their own paths toward authentic selfhood, mutual appreciation, and respect. As has been seen, biblical women are often represented as significant persons and important members of their communities, regardless of their marital status.

CARING FOR OTHERS AND THE COMMUNITY, OR "EVERY MAN FOR HIMSELF"?

Biblical traditions recall the deeds of many women who acted decisively and effectively on behalf of both themselves and others in the community.[8] Unlike the contemporary ideal—or idol—of the entrepreneur or "self-made man," most of these women, while certainly enterprising, as well as courageous, were not simply out to advance their own interests. Instead, their actions were meant to contribute to the well-being of other persons and of the larger communities in which they lived. Similarly, a variety

6. See above, chapters 1 and 2.

7. As to the recurrent tendency to adapt Christian norms to conventional secular standards, see H. R. Niebuhr's perennial pertinent *Christ and Culture*, especially chapter three describing the pattern Niebuhr characterizes as "the Christ of Culture" or "cultural Christianity."

8. See above, chapters 3 and 4.

of biblical traditions express positive appreciation for women in general, special respect for mothers, concern for daughters, and gratitude for good wives—as well as a husband's occasional complaining about life with one he found contentious or overbearing.[9]

Several biblical texts emphasize the importance of caring for widows and other vulnerable persons in the community. Laws intended to assist such persons can be characterized aptly as "biblical social welfare legislation," which provided them a kind of "safety net" or "social security" through a series of practical arrangements.[10] Throughout the Old Testament it is understood that YHWH was concerned with the welfare of his people. Biblical laws regularly give expression to this same concern.

Here, again, Old Testament law and practice can be contrasted with the modern ideology of autonomous (or "rugged") individualism. In its extreme form, proponents of this ideology insist that it is right to seek one's own advantage, but wrong to assist others except in exchange for equal value received.[11] According to this vision, life from cradle to grave, consists of a perpetual process of bargaining or trading value for value.[12] The tacit corollary is that social safety nets are anathema, and that people who are unable to pay their own way should be so obliging as to perish quietly, preferably out of sight, without disturbing the more fortunate.

---

9. See above, chapter 5.

10. See above, chapters 5 and 6.

11. This ideology comes to clear expression in the writings of Ayn Rand, particularly, in her book, *The Virtue of Selfishness*. See Sturm, *Solidarity and Suffering*, for a quite different vision of the human condition, emphasizing community, rather than "the individual." Robert Bellah and others have reflected on the peculiar difficulty Americans have explaining their involvement in community concerns on the basis of individual self-interest. Bellah, et al., *Habits of the Heart*. Reinhold Niebuhr's reflections on the themes of "the individual" and "community" are perhaps even more relevant to understanding and evaluating the American scene in the second decade of the Twenty-First Century than when he first set them down. See, e.g., Niebuhr, *Children of Light*, esp. chapter II; *Irony of American History*; and *Man's Nature and Communities*. See also Rebecca Hiers, "Leadership from the Heart," (reflecting on Native American values and practices), and Vowell, *Wordy Shipmates* (examining the modern relevance of Puritan ideals).

12. Wendell Berry draws a sketch of modern marriage grounded on such norms: "Marriage, in what is evidently its most popular version, is now on the one hand an intimate 'relationship' involving (ideally) two successful careerists in the same bed, and on the other hand a sort of private political system in which rights and interests must be constantly asserted and defended. Marriage, in other words, has now taken the form of divorce: a prolonged and impassioned negotiation as to how things shall be divided." *What are People For?*, 180.

Those who cannot pay their way, including children, the ill, disabled, unemployed, disaster victims, future generations, and all kinds of domestic animals and wildlife, do not count, since, necessarily, they are unable to exchange *quid pro quo* with present-day entrepreneurs.

It may be appropriate to mention that something like rugged individualism is said to have been at the root of the brutal anarchy, characterized by rape, murder, civil war, genocide and the nearly total disintegration of what had been the emerging nation of Israel that obtained during the latter part of the Period of the Judges: "In those days there was no king in Israel; every man did what was right in his own eyes."[13]

In our time, people who care about others are sometimes dismissed contemptuously as "bleeding hearts" or "left-leaning liberals." And persons who serve in helping professions such as school teachers, nurses, public defenders, and primary care physicians—whether male or female—are likely to be paid substantially less than those who undertake to advance their careers in more prestigious and remunerative vocations. The apparent rationale for such low esteem and compensation seems to be that helping others is considered less important than helping one's self.[14] Only a few decades ago, in the so-called McCarthy era, many Americans believed that people who were concerned about others in the community must be "communists," "socialists," and anyhow "un-American." It is significant that there is no basis in biblical tradition for the notion that there is something wrong or unworthy about caring for or serving the welfare of others and the larger community. Quite the contrary, as has been seen.[15]

13. Judges 17–21 describe the course of gruesome events during those chaotic years (approx. 1200–1000 BCE). The thematic statement quoted here (Judg 17:6 and 21:25) frames or brackets the book's account of these events. The biblical narrator-commentator clearly condemned and expected readers to condemn the atrocities against women (and men) described in these pages.

14. The same is generally the case as to people in "service" occupations, such as: farm workers, fire fighters, grocery clerks, hotel and motel "housekeepers," janitors, police officers, postal workers, restaurant and fast food waiters and waitresses, street cleaners, and trash collectors.

15. See also Wright, *God's People*, 260–65, discussing OT laws regarding property which embody "moral principles and social objectives" that may be applicable in "different but comparable modern contexts." Ibid., 261. See also Wright, *Walking in the Ways*, 13–45, on "the use of the Bible in social ethics." Also, more recently, Williams, "Adding Insult to Injury?," 106: "Although Deuteronomy does not attempt a thoroughgoing critique of its society, it does lay down principles by which oppression may be deconstructed . . . It does not mandate a philosophical, social, or political system that will

THE STATUS OF WOMEN AND WOMEN'S RIGHTS

Although many Americans still believe in progress, and many important advances have occurred in the area of civil rights, prejudicial attitudes and practices continue to disadvantage women in our society.[16] In the last hundred years, federal wage and hours laws have limited employers' ability to exploit and abuse women and children in the work place. Thanks to the Nineteenth Amendment, ratified over ninety years ago, women now have the right to vote. And in recent decades, Congress and the courts have acknowledged that adult married women have legal capacity to buy or rent property, obtain loans and credit cards, and engage in other contractual transactions without requiring their husbands' co-signatures.[17] Title VII of the Civil Rights Act of 1964 bars employers from discriminating against employees on the basis of gender in many employment settings,[18] and since 1986, affords some protection from sexual harassment in the workplace.[19] And Title IX of the Education Amendments of 1972[20] bans discrimination based on gender in educational institutions receiving federal funding. Sexual harassment is also actionable under Title IX.[21]

Nevertheless, invidious gender-based discrimination lingers on. As recently as 2011, a number of universities were under investigation for possible Title IX violations, including sexual harassment and sexual assault.[22] Moreover, judges are sometimes unwilling to recognize Title VII or Title IX claims when they see them,[23] or to order appropriate relief

---

bring this about. But its principle is clear: God does not want people to be poor, or to be rich at the expense of others."

16. Unequal, indeed, brutal treatment of women continues to be commonplace in many other "modern" nations. See *Newsweek*, Sept. 26, 2011, especially the following articles: "The Worst Places to Be a Woman," 32–33; Toni Morrison, "Dignity and Depravity," 42–43, and Michelle Goldberg, "Marry—or Else," 48–51.

17. See Collins, *When Everything Changed*, 22–23, 207, 250–51. As to women's legal capacity in biblical times, see above, chapters 8 through 11.

18. 42 U.S.C. sect, 2000e *et seq.* (1964) and as amended. See Collins, *When Everything Changed*, 75–81.

19. *Meritor Savings Bank v. Vinson*, 477 U.S. 57 (1986).

20. 20 U.S.C. 1681 *et seq.* (1972) and as amended.

21. See Hiers, "Sexual Harassment."

22. Among others, Duke University, Harvard Law School, Princeton, University of Virginia, and Yale. See Allan, "Confusion and Silence," 39–40.

23. See, e.g., *Harris v. Forklift Systems*, 510 U.S. 17 (1993) (reversing lower court holding that abusive workplace environment was not hostile enough to justify plaintiff's Title

when clearly justified.[24] When denying relief, courts often have done so on the tacit, and sometimes expressed, ground that to rule in plaintiffs' favor would be too costly or inconvenient to defendant businesses or corporations.[25] There were no business organizations or corporations in biblical times; however, no biblical texts justify denying vulnerable people justice just because doing them justice might be costly or inconvenient to the wealthy.

Although increasing numbers of women are now entering such professions as law and medicine, and more are being appointed corporate CEOs and directors, overall, women's income levels continue to lag behind those of their male counterparts. In all its history, the U.S. House of Representatives has elected just one woman as Speaker; and no woman has yet been chosen as U.S. Senate President.[26] Or as President or Vice President of the United States. A record total of three women new serve as Associate Justices of the U.S. Supreme Court—three out of nine. But only four, including these three, have ever done so in the Court's well over two hundred year history; and none has yet been appointed Chief Justice.[27] There has never been a woman Pope, nor is there likely to be one in the foreseeable future; and, though growing numbers of women have

---

VII claim); and *Waltman v. International Paper*, 875 F.2d 468, 482–87 (5th Cir. 1989) (dissent by Judge Edith Jones).

24. See, e.g., *Great American Fed. Sav. & Loan Ass'n v. Novotny*, 442 U.S. 366 (1979) (holding Title VII the "exclusive remedy" and therefore denying plaintiff's 42 U.S.C. sect. 1985(3) conspiracy claim); *Gebser v. Lago Vista Indep. Sch. Dist.*, 524 U.S. 274 (1998) (student could not sue under Title IX for sexual harassment by teacher when school officials lacked actual notice); *Ledbetter v. Goodyear Tire*, 127 S.Ct. 2162 (2007) (holding female employee could not sue under Title VII because she had failed to discover that she was underpaid compared to male coworkers and bring suit within 180 days of employer's first discriminatory act); and *Wal-Mart Stores v. Dukes*, 131 S.Ct. 2541 (2011) (denying class action certification for women claiming gender-based discrimination in violation of Title VII). See especially Green, "Insular Individualism," critiquing the Court's *Ledbetter* decision.

25. Courts also sometimes cite the prospect of future crowded dockets as reason for denying such plaintiffs' claims. The implication is that courts should save judicial resources for dealing with more important matters.

26. Until 1948, no woman had ever been elected to the U.S. Senate. There were only two, in 1972, and none the year following. There were then only thirteen women members of the House of Representatives. See Collins, *When Everything Changed*, 80–81, 251.

27. In all its history until 1979 when Carolyn Dineen Randall and Phyllis Kravitz were appointed by President Carter, no woman had ever served on the United States Court of Appeals for the Fifth Federal Circuit. Couch, *History*, 210. The first woman to

been ordained as ministers and rabbis in the United States, they remain in the minority. Never in its more than 300-year history has Yale University had a woman President; and its Divinity School, to date only one woman as Dean. The present author's other alma mater, the University of Florida, during its over 150 years, has not yet had a woman President, nor its Law School, a woman Dean.

Few women ascended to leadership positions in Old Testament times, either. But those who did, attained the highest levels of authority. As "judge," Deborah was a powerful and highly respected ruler of Israel, long before Israel had kings. Later, Jezebel and Athaliah, reigned as queens, respectively, over the kingdoms of Israel and Judah. To date, no women have risen to comparable positions of authority and responsibility in the United States.[28] In biblical times, there were no women priests. Yet the few, albeit very few, biblical women who were recognized as important prophets, continue to offer inspiration as role models for women's leadership in churches, synagogues, and seminaries.

As has been seen, biblical laws set out a number of rights, at least as the converse or correlatives of various mandated duties or obligations.[29] Some of these rights pertained to women. Several additional laws provided or protected the rights and interests of both men and women. To the extent that they did so, such laws can be recognized as expressions of the principle known in modern Anglo-American jurisprudence as "the equal protection of the laws."[30] The Fourteenth Amendment to the United States Constitution provides, among other protections: "No State shall . . . deny to any person within its jurisdiction the equal protection of the laws."[31] However, American courts apply a standard of review that is more

---

serve on the Florida Supreme Court, Justice (and later Chief Justice) Rosemary Barkett, was appointed in 1985.

28. In recent years, three women have served as Secretaries of State, and a few more in other Cabinet offices. Increasing numbers of women have been elected state governors.

29. See above, chapter 6.

30. See above, chapter 7.

31. U.S. Constitution, Article XIV, Section 1. American courts have held that the Due Process Clause of the Constitution's Fifth Amendment includes an "implied" Equal Protection Clause that applies to actions by the Federal government. The Constitution's Equal Protection Clause may be understood as giving legal expression to the Declaration of Independence affirmation that "all men are created equal." This affirmation, arguably derived, at least indirectly, from OT belief in human equality, a belief most notably expressed in the declaration that the primordial man and woman, from whom all humanity

deferential to government actions involving gender based discrimination than in cases of discrimination based on race, ethnicity, or national origin.[32] Some decades ago, proponents of the "Equal Rights Amendment" undertook thereby to correct this disparity. It may be recalled that the requisite number of state legislatures failed, by just three, to ratify this proposed amendment. And there is little prospect of reviving it now, given the present politically "conservative" culture.

It can be said, in conclusion, that the biblical ideal of gender equality under the law was not fully extended to all kinds of social contexts in biblical times. Yet in contrast to both classical and naturalistic humanism which tend to view male superiority as part of the natural order, biblical humanism, at its best, affirms the equal worth of persons, whether male or female. This biblical ideal—however imperfectly realized in its own time—continues to be an inspired and inspiring vision awaiting fuller actualization in many areas of law and social practice in the world today.

---

was said to have been descended, were both created in the image of God (Gen 1:26–27; 5:1–2; 9:6). At any rate, it is clear that, notwithstanding its naturalistic and rationalistic characterization as a "self-evident truth," the affirmation "all men are created equal" is a statement of faith and value. See H. R. Niebuhr, *Radical Monotheism*, chapter V, discussing "the democratic dogma of equality." To the extent that the "democratic dogma of equality" is grounded in the biblical affirmation that both men and women were created in the image of God, it can be understood to apply to all human beings, male and female alike.

32. In contrast to cases involving alleged discrimination against classes of persons where governmental justifications are reviewed under the "strict scrutiny" standard, governmental defenses in cases involving gender-based equal protection claims are reviewed using only "intermediate" scrutiny. See Robert Bork, responding to question by Lloyd Grove asking "Do you still believe the equal protection clause of the 14th Amendment should not apply to women?" Bork's answer: "Yeah. Women are a majority of the population now. They aren't discriminated against anymore." *Newsweek* (Oct. 24, 2011) 18. See generally O'Connor, "Legal Status of Women." Strangely, Justice O'Connor does not mention here this double standard of judicial review.

Bibliography

Allan, Nicole. "Confusion and Silence." *Yale Alumni Magazine* (July/August 2011) 39–42.

Arndt, Emily. *Demanding our Attention: The Hebrew Bible as a Source for Christian Ethics.* Grand Rapids: Eerdmans, 2011.

Attridge, Harold W. "Early Christians and the Care of the Poor." *Reflections: Yale Divinity School* (Fall, 2010) 14–17.

Beckmann, David. "A New Exodus from Hunger." *Reflections: Yale Divinity School* (Fall, 2010) 47–51.

Bellah, Robert, et al. *Habits of the Heart: Individualism and Commitment in American Life.* Rev. ed. San Francisco: HarperSanFrancisco, 1996.

Berkovits, Eliezer. *Jewish Women in Time and Torah.* Hoboken, NJ: KTAV, 1990.

Berman, Harold J. *Law and Revolution: The Formation of the Western Legal Tradition.* Cambridge: Harvard University Press, 1983.

Berry, Wendell. *What Are People For?* New York: North Point, 1990.

Biale, Rachel. *Women and Jewish Law: The Essential Texts, Their History, and Their Relevance for Today.* New York: Schocken, 1995.

Bird, Phyllis. "Images of Women in the Old Testament." In *Religion and Sexism: Images of Woman in the Jewish and Christian Traditions*, edited by Rosemary Radford Ruether, 41–88. New York: Simon & Schuster, 1974.

Boecker, Hans Jochen. *Law and the Administration of Justice in the Old Testament and Ancient East.* Translated by Jeremy Moiser. Minneapolis, MN: Augsburg, 1980.

Brin, Gershon. *Studies in Biblical Law: From the Hebrew Bible to the Dead Sea Scrolls.* JSOTSup 176. Translated by Jonathan Chipman. Sheffield, UK: Sheffield Academic, 1994.

Brueggemann, Walter. *Disruptive Grace: Reflections on God, Scripture, and the Church.* Edited and introduction by Carolyn J. Sharp. Minneapolis, MN: Fortress, 2011.

Burrows, Millar. *The Basis of Israelite Marriage.* American Oriental Series 15. New Haven, CT: American Oriental Society, 1939.

———. "The Marriage of Boaz and Ruth," *JBL* 59 (1940) 445–48.

———. *An Outline of Biblical Theology.* Philadelphia: Westminster, 1946.

Cahill, Lisa Sowle. *Between the Sexes: Foundations for a Christian Ethics of Sexuality.* Philadelphia: Fortress, 1983.

———. *Sex, Gender and Christian Ethics.* Cambridge: Cambridge University Press, 1996.

Carmichael, Calum. *The Spirit of Biblical Law.* Athens, GA: University of Georgia Press, 1996.

Carmody, Denise Lardner. *Biblical Woman: Contemporary Reflections on Scriptural Texts.* New York: Crossroad, 1988.

Cohn, Haim H. *Human Rights in the Bible and Talmud.* Tel Aviv: MOD, 1989.

———. *Human Rights in Jewish Law.* New York: KTAV, 1984.

Collins, Gail. *When Everything Changed: The Amazing Journey of American Women from 1960 to the Present.* New York: Little, Brown, & Co., 2009.

Coogan, Michael D., ed. *The New Oxford Annotated Bible, with the Apocryphal / Deuterocanonical Books.* 3rd ed. New Revised Standard Version. New York: Oxford University Press, 2001.

Corbin, Arthur Linton. *Corbin on Contracts.* Vol. 1. Rev. ed. Edited by Joseph M. Perillo. St. Paul, MN: West, 1993.

Couch, Harvey C. *A History of the Fifth Circuit, 1891–1981.* Washington, DC: Bicentennial Committee of the Judicial Conference of the United States, 1984.

Crenshaw, James L., and John T. Willis, eds. *Essays in Old Testament Ethics.* New York: KTAV, 1974.

Daube, David. *Ancient Jewish Law.* Leiden: Brill, 1981.

Davidman, Lynn, and Shelly Tenenbaum, eds. *Feminist Perspectives on Jewish Studies.* New Haven, CT: Yale University Press, 1994.

Davidson, B. *The Analytical Hebrew and Chaldee Lexicon.* New York: Harper, 1959.

Day, Peggy L., ed. *Gender and Difference in Ancient Israel.* Minneapolis: Fortress, 1989.

Ebeling, Jennie R. *Women's Lives in Biblical Times.* London: T. & T. Clark, 2010.

Evans, Mary J. *Woman in the Bible: An Overview of all the Crucial Passages on Women's Roles.* Downers Grove, IL: InterVarsity, 1983.

Exum, J. Cheryl. "'Mother in Israel': A Familiar Figure Reconsidered." In *Feminist Interpretation of the Bible,* edited by Letty M. Russell, 73–85. Philadelphia: Westminster, 1985.

Falk, Ze'ev W. *Law and Religion: The Jewish Experience.* Jerusalem: Mesharim, 1981.

Fiorenza, Elizabeth Schüssler. "Interpreting Patriarchal Traditions." In *The Liberating Word: A Guide to Nonsexist Interpretation of the Bible,* edited by Letty M. Russell, 39–61. Philadelphia: Westminster, 1976.

Frymer-Kensky, Tikva. "The Bible and Women's Studies." In *Feminist Perspectives on Jewish Studies,* edited by Lynn Davidman and Shelly Tenenbaum, 16–39. New Haven, CT: Yale University Press, 1994.

———. *Reading the Women of the Bible: A New Interpretation of their Stories.* New York; Schocken, 2002.

———. "Virginity in the Bible." In *Gender and Law in the Hebrew Bible and the Ancient Near East,* JSOTSup 262, edited by Victor H. Matthews et al., 79–96. Sheffield, UK: Sheffield Academic, 1998.

Fuchs, Esther. *Sexual Politics in the Biblical Narrative: Reading the Hebrew Bible as a Woman.* JSOTSup 310. Sheffield, UK: Sheffield Academic, 2000.

Garner, Bryan A., ed. *Black's Law Dictionary.* 8th ed. Minneapolis: West, 2004.

Goldberg, Michelle. "Marry—or Else: 'Honor Killings' in the United States." *Newsweek,* September 26, 2011, 48–51.

Green, Tristin K. "Insular Individualism: Employment Discrimination Law after Ledbetter v. Goodyear." *Harvard Civil Rights—Civil Liberties Law Review* 43 (2008) 353.

Gunkel, Hermann. *The Legends of Genesis: The Biblical Saga and History.* New York: Schocken, 1964.

Hiebert, Paula S. "'Whence Shall Help Come to Me?': The Biblical Widow." In *Gender and Difference in Ancient Israel,* edited by Peggy L. Day, 125–41. Minneapolis: Fortress, 1989.

Hiers, Rebecca H. "Leadership from the Heart: One Tribe's Example." *Journal of Law and Religion* 26 (2011) 541–83.

Hiers, Richard H. "*Ancient Laws, Yet Strangely Modern: Biblical Contract and Tort Jurisprudence.*" *University of Detroit Mercy Law Review* 88 (2011) 473–96.

————. "Biblical Social Welfare Legislation." *Journal of Law and Religion* 17 (2002) 49–96.

————. *Jesus and Ethics. Four Interpretations: Adolf von Harnack, Albert Schweitzer, Rudolf Bultmann, C. H. Dodd.* Philadelphia: Westminster, 1968.

————. *Jesus and the Future: Unresolved Questions for Understanding and Faith.* Atlanta: John Knox, 1981.

————. *Justice and Compassion in Biblical Law.* New York: Continuum, 2009.

————. "Reverence for Life and Environmental Ethics in Biblical Law and Covenant." *Journal of Law and Religion* 13 (1996–98) 127–88. Revised and re-published in *Forum on Religion and Ecology*: http://fore.research.yale.edu/religion/christianity/essays/chris_hiers_index.html

————. "Sexual Harassment: Title VII and Title IX Protections and Prohibitions—The Current State of the Law." *Annual of the Society of Christian Ethics* 19 (1999) 391–406.

————. "Transfer of Property by Inheritance and Bequest in Biblical Law and Tradition." *Journal of Law and Religion* 10 (1993–94) 121–55.

————. *The Trinity Guide to the Bible.* Harrisburg, PA: Trinity, 2001.

Hollyday, Joyce. *Clothed with the Sun: Biblical Women, Social Justice, and Us.* Louisville: Westminster John Knox, 1994.

Hurley, James B. *Man and Woman in Biblical Perspective.* Grand Rapids: Zondervan, 1981.

Jay, Nancy B. *Throughout Your Generations Forever: Sacrifice, Religion, and Paternity.* Chicago: University Chicago Press, 1992.

Kent, Grenville. "His Desire is For Her: Feminist Readings in the Song of Solomon." In *Tamar's Tears: Evangelical Engagements with Feminist Old Testament Hermeneutics,* edited by Andrew Sloane, 217–48. Eugene, OR: Pickwick, 2012.

Keys, Arthur B., Jr., "The Poor We'll Always Have?" *Reflections: Yale Divinity School* (Fall, 2010) 11–13.

LaFave, Wayne R. *Criminal Law.* 3d ed. St. Paul, MN: West Group, 2000.

Levine, Baruch A. "In Praise of the Israelite *Mishpacha*: Legal Themes in the Book of Ruth." In *The Quest for the Kingdom of God: Studies in Honor of George E. Mendenhall,* edited by H. B. Huffmon, et al, 95–106. Winona Lake, IN: Eisenbrauns, 1983.

Malchow, Bruce V. *Social Justice in the Hebrew Bible.* Collegeville, MN: Liturgical, 1996.

Maston, T. B. *Biblical Ethics.* Macon, GA: Mercer University Press, 1982.

Matthews, Victor H., et al., eds. *Gender and Law in the Hebrew Bible and the Ancient Near East.* JSOTSup 262. Sheffield, UK: Sheffield Academic, 1998.

May, Herbert G., and Bruce M. Metzger, eds., *The New Oxford Annotated Bible with the Apocrypha.* Revised Standard Version, Containing the Second Edition of the New Testament and an Expanded Edition of the [Old Testament] Apocrypha. New York: Oxford University Press, 1977.

Mickle, Shelly Fraser. *Replacing Dad.* Chapel Hill, NC: Algonquin, 1993.

Morrison, Toni. "Dignity and Depravity." *Newsweek,* September 26, 2011, 42–43.

Muir, William K., Jr. *Law and Attitude Change.* Chicago: University of Chicago Press, 1984.

Niebuhr, H. Richard. *Christ and Culture.* New York: Harper and Row, 1956.

————. *Radical Monotheism and Western Culture.* With Supplementary Essays. Louisville: Westminster/John Knox, 1993.

Niebuhr, Reinhold. *Children of Light and Children of Darkness.* New York: Scribner's, 1944.

————. *The Irony of American History.* New York: Scribner's, 1952.

————. *Man's Nature and His Communities*. New York: Scribner's, 1965.

O'Connor, Sandra Day. "The Legal Status of Women: the Journey Toward Equality." *Journal of Law and Religion* 15 (2000–2001) 29–36.

Otto, Eckart. "False Weights in the Scales of Biblical Justice? Different Views of Women from Patriarchal Hierarchy to Religious Equality in the Book of Deuteronomy." In *Gender and Law in the Hebrew Bible and the Ancient Near East*, JSOTSup 262, edited by Victor H. Matthews, et al., 128–46. Sheffield, UK: Sheffield Academic, 1998.

Parry, Robin A. "Feminist Hermeneutics and Evangelical Concerns: The Rape of Dinah as a Case Study." In *Tamar's Tears: Evangelical Engagements with Feminist Old Testament Hermeneutics*, edited by Andrew Sloane, 30–64. Eugene, OR: Pickwick, 2012.

Patrick, Dale. *Old Testament Law*. Atlanta: John Knox, 1985.

Pilch, John J., and Bruce J. Malina. *Biblical Social Values and their Meaning*. Peabody, MA: Hendrickson, 1993.

Plaskow, Judith. *Standing Again at Sinai: Judaism from a Feminist Perspective*. New York: Harper & Row, 1990.

Pokrifka, Junia. "Patriarchy, Biblical Authority, and the Grand Narrative of the Old Testament." In *Tamar's Tears: Evangelical Engagements with Feminist Old Testament Hermeneutics*, edited by Andrew Sloane, 274–314. Eugene, OR: Pickwick, 2012.

Pressler, Carolyn. *The View of Women Found in the Deuteronomic Family Laws*. Beihefte zur Zeitschrift für die alttestamentliche Wissenschaft 216. Berlin: de Gruyter, 1993.

————. "Wives and Daughters, Bond and Free: Views of Women in the Slave Laws of Exodus 21:2–11." In *Gender and Law in the Hebrew Bible and the Ancient Near East*, JSOTSup 262, edited by Victor H. Matthews et al., 147–72. Sheffield, UK: Sheffield Academic, 1998.

Prusak, Bernard P. "Woman: Seductive Siren and Source of Sin?" In *Religion and Sexism: Images of Woman in the Jewish and Christian Traditions*, edited by Rosemary Radford Ruether, 89–116. New York: Simon & Schuster, 1974.

Rand, Ayn. *The Virtue of Selfishness: A New Concept of Egoism*. With Additional Essays by Nathaniel Brandon. New York: New American Library, 1964.

Ruether, Rosemary Radford ed. *Religion and Sexism: Images of Woman in the Jewish and Christian Traditions*. New York: Simon & Schuster, 1974.

Russell, Letty M., ed. *Feminist Interpretation of the Bible*. Philadelphia: Westminster, 1985.

————. *The Liberating Word: A Guide to Nonsexist Interpretation of the Bible*. Philadelphia: Westminster, 1976.

Sanders, Jack T. *Ethics in the New Testament*. Philadelphia: Fortress, 1975.

Sasson, Jack M. *Ruth: A New Translation with Philological Commentary and a Formalist-Folklorist Interpretation*. Baltimore: Johns Hopkins University Press, 1979.

Schaberg, Jane. "New Testament: The Case of Mary Magdalene." In *Feminist Approaches to the Bible*, edited by Phyllis Trible et al., 75–91. Washington, DC: Biblical Archeology Society, 1995.

Scholz, Suzanne. *Introducing the Women's Hebrew Bible*. Introductions in Feminist Theology 13. London: T. & T. Clark, 2007.

Schottroff, Luise, et al. *Feminist Interpretation: The Bible in Women's Perspective*. Minneapolis: Fortress, 1998.

————. "Toward a Feminist Reconstruction of the History of Early Christianity." In *Feminist Interpretation: the Bible in Women's Perspective*, edited by Luise Schottroff et al., 179–254. Minneapolis: Fortress, 1998.

Schroer, Silvia. "Toward a Feminist Reconstruction of the History of Israel." In *Feminist Interpretation: The Bible in Women's Perspective*, edited by Luise Schottroff et al., 85–176. Minneapolis: Fortress, 1998.

Sharp, Carolyn J. *Wrestling the Word: The Hebrew Scriptures and the Christian Believer.* Louisville: Westminster John Knox, 2011.

Sloane, Andrew. "'And he shall rule over you': Evangelists, Feminists and Genesis 2–3." In *Tamar's Tears: Evangelical Engagements with Feminist Old Testament Hermeneutics*, edited by Andrew Sloane, 1–29. Eugene, OR: Pickwick, 2012.

Sölle, Dorothee. *Great Women of the Bible in Art and Literature.* Translated by Joe H. Kirchberger. Grand Rapids: Eerdmans, 1994.

Starr, Lee Anna. *The Bible Status of Woman: Women in American Protestant Religion, 1800–1930 Series.* 1926. Reprint. New York: Garland, 1987.

Steinberg, Naomi. *Kinship and Marriage in Genesis: A Household Economics Perspective.* Minneapolis: Fortress, 1998.

Stendahl, Krister. *The Bible and the Role of Women: A Case Study in Hermeneutics.* Philadelphia: Fortress, 1966.

Sturm, Douglas. *Solidarity and Suffering: Toward a Politics of Relationality.* Albany, NY: State of New York University Press, 1998.

Trible, Phyllis, "The Bible in Transit." *Reflections: Yale Divinity School* (Spring, 2011) 31–33.

———. "Eve and Miriam: from the Margins to the Center." In *Feminist Approaches to the Bible*, edited by Phyllis Trible, et al., 5–24. Washington, DC: Biblical Archeology Society, 1995.

——— et al., *Feminist Approaches to the Bible.* Washington, DC: Biblical Archeology Society, 1995.

———. *God and the Rhetoric of Sexuality.* Philadelphia: Fortress, 1978.

———. *Texts of Terror.* Philadelphia: Fortress, 1984.

Vowell, Sarah. *The Wordy Shipmates.* New York: Riverhead, 2008.

Wacker, Marie-Theres. "Historical, Hermeneutical, and Methodological Foundations." In *Feminist Interpretation: The Bible in Women's Perspective*, edited by Luise Schottroff, et al., 3–82. Minneapolis: Fortress, 1998.

Westbrook, Raymond. "The Female Slave." In *Gender and Law in the Hebrew Bible and the Ancient Near East.* JSOTSup 262, edited by Victor H. Matthews et al., 214–38. Sheffield, UK: Sheffield Academic, 1998.

———. *Property and the Family in Biblical Law.* JSOTSup 113. Sheffield, UK: Sheffield Academic, 1991.

Westbrook, Raymond, and Bruce Wells. *Everyday Law in Biblical Israel: An Introduction.* Louisville: Westminster John Knox, 2009.

Wilder, Amos N. *Eschatology and Ethics in the Teachings of Jesus.* New York: Harper, 1950.

Williams, Jenni. "Adding Insult to Injury? The Family Laws of Deuteronomy." In *Tamar's Tears: Evangelical Engagements with Feminist Old Testament Hermeneutics*, edited by Andrew Sloane, 84–111. Eugene, OR: Pickwick, 2012.

Wolfson, Susan A. "Modern Liberal Rights Theory and Jewish Law." *Journal of Law and Religion* 9 (1992) 399–428.

Wright, Christopher J. H. *God's People in God's Land.* Exeter, UK: Paternoster, 1990.

———. *Old Testament Ethics for the People of God.* Downer's Grove, IL: InterVarsity, 2004.

———. *Walking in the Ways of the Lord: The Ethical Authority of the Old Testament.* Leicester, UK: Apollos, 1995.

Index of Scripture

~

Index of Names

Aaron, 18
Abigail, 9–10, 22, 27, 81
Abimelech, 16, 17
Abraham, Abram, ix, xxii, 3–5, 7, 37, 53, 79
Absalom, 17, 60, 61
Achsah, 64
Adah, 9
Adam, 35–36, 80
Adonijah, 11
Ahab, 9, 12, 19, 53
Ahasuerus, 19, 23–25
Ahaziah, 19
Alexandra, 19
Allan, Nicole, 90
Amnon, ix, 54
Anna (NT), 18
Anna (OT), 9, 12–13, 81
Arndt, Emily, xxi, xxii
Asa, 20
Athaliah, 19, 82, 92
Attridge, Harold W., xxi

Balaam, 29
Barak, 16
Barkett, Justice Rosemary, 92
Bathsheba, 9–11, 20, 30, 60, 64, 81
Beckmann, David, xxi
Bellah, Robert, 88
Berkovits, Eliezer, 50
Berman, Harold J., 85
Berry, Wendell, 88
Biale, Rachel, 50, 53
Bilhah, 4, 6
Bird, Phyllis, 27, 29, 33, 36, 81

Boaz, 23, 66, 73–76
Boecker, Hans Jochen, 37, 56, 57, 59–61, 75
Bork, Judge Robert, 93
Brin, Gershon, 42
Brueggemann, Walter, 25
Bultmann, Rudolf, xxiv
Burrows, Millar, 37, 40, 48, 54, 71, 75, 77

Cahill, Lisa Sowle, ix–xii, 1, 27, 29
Cannon, Katie Geneva, 1
Carmichael, Calum, xxiv
Carmody, Denise Lardner, 38, 54, 61
Carter, President Jimmy, 91
Chilion, 73–75, 80
Chloe, xi
Cohn, Haim H., 50
Collins, Gail, 90, 91
Corbin, Arthur Linton, 63
Couch, Harvey C., 91
Crenshaw, James L., xxii

Daniel, 26, 56
Darius, 29
Daube, David, 74
David, 3, 8–11, 17, 23, 25, 30, 31, 53, 54, 60, 61, 64, 86
Davidman, Lynn, 50
Davidson, B., 45, 47
Deborah, x, xiii, 16, 18, 22, 27, 56, 82, 92
Delilah, 16–18
Dodd, C. H., xxiv
Dugard, Jaycee, ix

Subject Index

Tanakh, xvii, 20
  See also Hebrew Bible, Jewish
    Scripture(s)
Ten Commandments. *See* Decalogue
Tenth Commandment, 37, 52
teraphim, 7
testimony by women, 56–62
third year tithe, 41–42, 46
Title VII, 90–91
Title IX, 90–91
tokens of virginity, 59–60
torts, xvi
  damages, 60
  defamation, 60
  personal injury, 51
  to pregnant women, 47
  to slaves, 51
  tort laws, 51
treason, 12
trusteeship. *See* property

unequal protection, 53–55
ungovernable son law, 55, 58–59
Unjust Judge parable, 62, 83
United States Constitution, 92–93
United States Court of Appeals,
  Fifth Judicial Circuit, 91–92

values
  societal or cultural, xxvi, 44, 81,
    87–89
  See also contemporary society
virgin, -ity, ix, 34, 35, 54, 59–60
vows
  religious vows, 34–35, 40, 50
  others, 34, 40, 50, 78–79
Vulgate, xviii, 4
vulnerable persons, 83, 88, 91

"weaker sex," 20–21
welfare legislation, 41–42, 46, 82, 86
  levirate marriage. *See* levirate
    marriage
  safety net. *See* safety net

share in festivals. *See* harvest
  festivals
third year tithe. *See* third year
  tithe
  See also entitlements, equal pro-
    tection, food banks, gleaning,
    safety net, social security
Western law / jurisprudence, 42, 85
  See also Anglo-American law /
    jurisprudence
Western literature, 85
WIC, 41
widow(s), xiii, 7–8, 40–42
  abuse or affliction of, 40, 41,
    45–46, 77–78
  access to courts, 57–58, 62
  asserting rights, 7–8, 56–58, 62
  beneficiaries of wills, 64
  clothing of, 46
  gleaning privileges. *See* gleaning
  inherit property, xiii, 71–80, 84
  own property, 40, 64–65, 68–69,
    73–80
  as property, 40
  protections for, 41–42, 45–46,
    82, 83
  rights of, 7–8, 41, 46–48, 56–57,
    62, 83
  sold as slaves, 40
  welfare of, 40–42, 86
wife, wives, 35–40
  "brawling" (or contentious), 39,
    82
  contempt for husbands, 24
  determined personalities, xxxiii,
    1, 3–13, 81, 87
  dominant spouse, 3–7, 36
  "evil" wives, 39
  "good" wives, 37–38, 64, 82
  Hittite, 6
  housewives, 87
  Job's, 13
  neighbor's, 36–37
  obsequious, 81